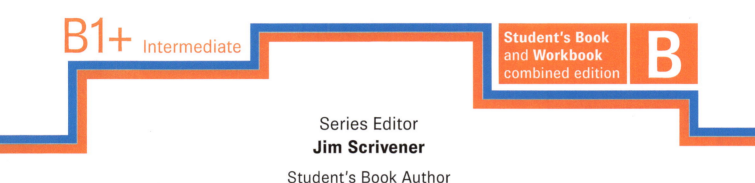

Personal Best

B1+ Intermediate

Student's Book
and **Workbook**
combined edition

B

Series Editor
Jim Scrivener

Student's Book Author
Graham Burton

Workbook Authors
Elizabeth Walter
and **Kate Woodford**

Richmond

STUDENT'S BOOK CONTENTS

Language App, unit-by-unit grammar and vocabulary games

UNIT 7

Entertainment

LANGUAGE the passive ■ movies

7A Lights, camera, action!

1 A Match the types of movies in the box with pictures a–d.

> animation   action movie
> horror movie   romantic comedy

B Have you seen any of these types of movies recently? Which movies did you see?

Go to Vocabulary practice: movies, page 146

2 Look at the picture in the text. What type of movie is *The Martian*? Would you like to see it?

HELP IS ONLY 140 MILLION MILES AWAY

MATT DAMON
THE MARTIAN

IN CINEMAS SEPTEMBER 30 IN 3D

THE MARTIAN

Plot

The year is 2035. A team of astronauts is sent on a mission to Mars, but a storm forces them to abandon their mission and fly back to Earth. As they are preparing to leave, astronaut Mark Watney, played by Matt Damon, disappears. The team thinks he has been killed, so they leave without him. When NASA realizes he has survived, they organize a dangerous mission to save him before his supply of food, water, and oxygen runs out. Will he be rescued before it's too late?

NASA's involvement

Scientists at NASA worked closely with the director of *The Martian*, giving advice about the science behind space travel and the technology needed to survive on Mars. Jessica Chastain, who plays the commander of the Mars mission in the movie, spent time with astronaut Tracy Caldwell Dyson to learn more about life in space. Real missions to Mars are being planned for the 2040s, so NASA's advice was based on the latest research.

Interesting facts

* *The Martian* was directed by Ridley Scott, who has made other science-fiction movies, including *Alien* and *Blade Runner*.
* It was shot in Jordan because the desert is similar to the color of Mars.
* A few days before the movie was released, scientists discovered water on Mars.

3 Read the text. Are the sentences true (T) or false (F)?

1 In the movie, Watney survives the storm and NASA tries to rescue him.   _____
2 Jessica Chastain plays the astronaut Tracy Caldwell Dyson.   _____
3 NASA is planning to send astronauts to Mars in our lifetime.   _____
4 The director of *The Martian* was Matt Damon.   _____
5 In the movie, the astronauts find water on Mars.   _____

4 A What tenses and forms are the **bold** verbs in column A?

Column A		Column B
NASA **sends** a team of astronauts to Mars.	→	A team of astronauts ¹_____ to Mars.
NASA **is planning** real missions to Mars.	→	Real missions to Mars ²_____ .
The team thinks the storm **has killed** Watney.	→	The team thinks Watney ³_____ .
Ridley Scott **directed** *The Martian*.	→	*The Martian* ⁴_____ by Ridley Scott.
Will NASA **rescue** Watney before it's too late?	→	⁵_____ Watney _____ before it's too late?

58

B Complete the sentences in column B so they have the same meaning as the sentences in column A. Check your answers in the text.

5 **A** Look at the pairs of sentences in exercise 4A. Answer the questions.

    1 Which sentences use the active form of the verbs? Which use the passive?

    2 In column A, do we know who/what did the action of the verbs in **bold**? And in column B?

    B Complete the rules and answer the questions about the passive. Then read the Grammar box.

    1 We make the passive with the verb _____ and the _____ form of the main verb.

    2 We change the tense of the passive by changing the tense of _____ .

    3 What is more important: the action, or the person who did the action? _____

    4 If we want to say who/what did the action, which word do we use? _____

📖 **Grammar** **the passive**

Simple present:
*English **is spoken** here.*

Present perfect:
*My bag **has been stolen**!*

Simple past:
*The bridge **was built** in 2010.*

Future with *will*:
*My laptop **will be fixed** next week.*

Present continuous:
*That new movie **is being shown**.*

Go to Grammar practice: the passive, page 124

6 ▶7.5 **Pronunciation: past participles** Look at the past participles. Say how the vowel sounds are pronounced: /ow/, /ʌ/ or /ɔ/. Listen, check, and repeat.

    shown chosen won lost spoken known dubbed done

7 **A** Complete the text with verbs in the passive using the past participles in exercise 6.

Did you know …?

- When a movie ¹_____ , voice actors usually provide the dialogue in different languages, but sometimes the dubbing ²_____ by the original actors, for example, Jodie Foster (French) and Viggo Mortensen (Spanish).

- *The Martian* ³_____ on a screen in space shortly after it was released. Astronauts watched it on the International Space Station. Maybe one day, it will be watched on Mars!

- The name "Oscars" ⁴_____ by accident – an executive director of the Film Academy said the statues looked like her Uncle Oscar, and the name stuck! Since the awards began, about 3,000 Oscar awards ⁵_____ .

- It's surprising how many statues ⁶_____ ! Angelina Jolie hid hers and doesn't know where it is, and Matt Damon can't find his. Marlon Brando, who ⁷_____ best _____ for his role in *The Godfather*, lost both of his statues.

- Na'vi, the language created for the 2009 movie *Avatar*, ⁸_____ still _____ today! Fans learn new words and talk to other Na'vi speakers on learnnavi.org.

B ▶7.6 Listen and check. Practice saying the passive sentences with the correct pronunciation of the past participles.

Go to Communication practice: Student A page 161, Student B page 170

8 In pairs, talk about your favorite movie. Use the questions to help you.

- What type of movie is it?
- Who was it directed by?
- Who stars in the movie?
- What is the plot of the movie?

- Where and when is it set?
- Is it based on a true story or a novel?
- Does it have good special effects and a good soundtrack?
- Was the movie shown with subtitles or was it dubbed?

Personal Best Write five sentences with the passive about your favorite movie star.

7B Action man

1 A Who's your favorite actor or action hero? Why?

B Look at the picture in the text on page 61. What job does the man on the left do? Read the text quickly and check. What's his name?

> ### Skill   guessing the meaning of words from context
>
> You can sometimes guess what a word means by looking for clues in the word and in the sentence.
> • Look at the sentence and identify what type of word it is (verb, noun, adjective, etc.).
> • Identify any parts of the word that you already understand.
> • Look at the immediate context of the word in the clause and sentence, and look at the wider context of the word in the surrounding sentences.
> • After guessing the meaning, read the sentences again to see if your guess makes sense in context.

2 A Read the Skill box. Look at the **bold** words 1–6 in the text. What types of word are they?

B Choose the correct definition for the **bold** words. Underline the parts of the text that helped you guess the meaning from context.

1 a a dangerous car	**b** a movie director	**c** a dangerous action
2 a a camera	**b** where a movie is shot	**c** a screen
3 a body parts	**b** damage to your body	**c** responsibilities
4 a boring	**b** crazy	**c** fascinating
5 a amazing	**b** climbing	**c** jumping
6 a exciting	**b** falling	**c** dangerous

3 Read the text again and answer the questions.

1 Did the stunt in the first paragraph go well? Why was Vic worried?
2 Has Vic had a successful career? How do you know?
3 Who wrote a book about Vic?
4 How often does Vic get hurt in his job?
5 What do Vic's wife and children do?
6 When they were young, what kind of games did Vic play with his children?
7 Which movies does Vic have great memories of? Why?
8 What comparison is made between special effects and stunts?

4 Underline four other words in the text that you don't know. Can you guess their meaning from the surrounding context?

> ### Text builder   referencing: *this* and *that*
>
> We can use *this* and *that* to refer back to ideas that have already appeared in the text. The ideas can be nouns or whole phrases:
> *Vic has broken **his legs, an arm, his ribs, and his nose**. **This** is only the start of a long list of injuries.*
> ***Vic jumped from a running horse onto a moving tank**. **That** even amazed director Steven Spielberg.*

5 Read the Text builder. Look at the fourth paragraph of the text. Find one example of *this* and one of *that*. Do they refer back to nouns or phrases?

6 Discuss the questions in pairs.

1 Which movies have amazing special effects or stunts? Why are they amazing?
2 Would you like to be a stunt performer? Why/Why not?
3 What other jobs are there in the movie industry? Would you like to do any of them?

World's
greatest
stunt performer

The car raced forward. It was already on fire, but the driver never stopped. The vehicle went up a ramp, into the sky, and then crashed into a bus. Finally, the driver got out and walked away, happy with the [1]**stunt**. Although it had gone smoothly, it had been hard to watch for Vic Armstrong, the stunt director on the [2]**movie set**. The driver was his son, Scott, who was following in his father's footsteps in the most dangerous way possible.

Even though the general public has probably not heard of Vic Armstrong, everyone has certainly seen him in action because Vic is the world's greatest stunt performer. In his career, he has been the stunt double for almost every major Hollywood star, including Tom Cruise and Arnold Schwarzenegger, and he can play almost anyone as long as there's danger involved.

It's a life that has taken him all around the world. Armstrong has now written about his life in his autobiography, *The True Adventures of the World's Greatest Stuntman*, and it's a bone-crunching tale. In his career, Vic has broken his legs, an arm, his ribs, and his nose. This is only the start of a long list of [3]**injuries** – bumps and bruises are an everyday occurrence in his working day. There's never a [4]**dull** moment in his life of excitement, even if he himself admits that some of his stunts are a little risky, such as [5]**leaping** out of a moving helicopter onto the side of a mountain.

Fortunately, Vic doesn't work alone. His company, Armstrong Action, is a family affair. Vic met his wife, Wendy, when they were both stunt performers on *Superman 2*. At the time, she was substituting the superhero's girlfriend, Lois Lane. Vic, of course, was Superman. His son Scott and their other three children eventually went into the business, too. That's hardly surprising because they were encouraged to face danger from an early age. When Vic's kids were just five years old, he put a special airbag in their garden for the children. This was for a game which involved jumping out of the upstairs window!

Their childhood wasn't all play, however. Vic's daughter Georgina first appeared on screen at the age of four, and was working with Steven Spielberg on the *Indiana Jones* movies before her seventh birthday. The *Indiana Jones* movies remain a career highlight for Vic, too, and not just because he was the stunt double for megastar Harrison Ford (pictured above with Vic). In one stunt, which is probably one of his most famous ones, Vic jumped from a running horse onto a moving tank. That even amazed director Steven Spielberg.

No special effects or computer-generated images can truly recreate how [6]**thrilling** it is to see stunt performers jump off a building or set themselves on fire. Indeed, it is the work of people like Vic, Wendy, and their children that helps make these movies so exciting and realistic. Without people like the Armstrongs, there would be lights, camera … but no action!

7C Got talent

1 Complete the TV guide below with the types of programs in the box.

talent show   the news   game show   documentary

Tuesday	What's on …
18.30	**Make a Fortune!** The ¹_____ where contestants win $1,000 for each correct answer.
19.00	**Natural Focus** This week's nature ²_____ looks at the marine life in Antarctica.
20.00	³_____ **at 8** The latest stories from our reporters around the world.
21.00	**Sing! Sang! Sung!** It's the final of the popular ⁴_____ . Who will win the top prize?

Go to Vocabulary practice: TV and music, page 147

2 Answer the questions in pairs.

1 What types of shows do you like? What's your favorite TV series?
2 Who is your favorite singer or band? Have you ever seen them live?

3 A Look at the title of the text and the pictures. What type of show is it?

B Read the text. What talent do these two people have? What's unusual about their stories?

WHO'S GOT TALENT?

Got Talent has been shown in over 60 countries and is now the most popular talent show in the world.
Here are two unusual stories from two different countries.

Shaheen Jafargholi

Shaheen was 12 years old when he sang *Who's Lovin' You* by Michael Jackson on *Britain's Got Talent* and amazed the judges. He later received an invitation from the singer to perform during his "This Is It" tour. Tragically, Jackson died soon after, so Shaheen wasn't able to sing with his hero, but his family asked Shaheen to sing at Jackson's memorial concert in front of a TV audience of a billion people! He can act, too, having appeared in the soap opera *EastEnders*, and he'd like to be able to continue with his acting career in the future.

Jennifer Grout

The audience laughed when 23-year-old Jennifer Grout couldn't understand the question, "What's your name?" the first time she appeared on *Arabs Got Talent*. Jennifer couldn't speak Arabic, but she was able to sing a perfect version of *Baeed Annak* by the Egyptian singer, Umm Kulthum. One judge commented, "You can't speak a word of Arabic, but you can sing better than some Arab singers!" Jennifer was one of the three finalists, and she hopes that in the future, she'll be able to make an album of traditional Moroccan music.

4 A Match the two parts to make complete sentences. Check your answers in the text.

1 Jackson died before the tour, so Shaheen **wasn't able to**
2 Shaheen **can**
3 He'd like **to be able to**
4 The audience laughed when Jennifer **couldn't**
5 Jennifer couldn't speak Arabic, but she **was able to**
6 She hopes that in the future, she'**ll be able to**

a continue with his acting career.
b act, too.
c sing with his hero.
d sing a perfect version of *Baeed Annak*.
e understand the question, "What's your name?"
f make an album of traditional Moroccan music.

B Look at the sentences in 4A again and answer the questions. Then read the Grammar box.

1 Which tense or form are the words in **bold**? Match them with the forms below.

simple present _____   simple past   _____ , _____ , _____

future with *will* _____   infinitive form _____

2 Complete the rules with *can, could, be able to,* or *was able to.*

We use _____ for present ability and possibility.

We use _____ or _____ for past ability and possibility.

For other tenses and forms, we use _____ .

📖 **Grammar** | **modals of ability and possibility**

Ability:
*She **can** play the piano really well.*
*I **couldn't** swim when I was young.*
*I**'ll be able to** speak French one day.*
*Sam would like **to be able to** sing.*

Possibility:
*He **can't** come tonight because he's sick.*
*I **couldn't** wait because I was in a hurry.*
*I**'ll be able to** go skiing in the U.S.*
*I **haven't been able to** visit him yet.*

Look! We usually use **can** for the simple present and **could** for the simple past and conditional forms. We use **be able to** for other tenses and forms when it's not possible to use a form of *can*:

*After my exams, I**'ll be able to** relax.* NOT ~~I will can relax.~~

Go to **Grammar practice:** modals of ability and possibility, page 125

5 **A** ▶7.11 **Pronunciation:** /eɪ/ and /ʊ/ sounds Listen to the six sentences. Pay attention to the pronunciation of *able* and *could*.

1 I haven't been able to exercise today.
2 I've been able to drive since I was 17.
3 I won't be able to go out tonight.
4 I couldn't sleep late last weekend.
5 When I was young, I could play an instrument.
6 I couldn't understand the teacher earlier.

B ▶7.11 Listen again and repeat. Are the sentences true for you?

6 ▶7.12 Complete the text with the verbs in the box and the correct form of *can/could* where possible, or *be able to.* Then listen and check.

> play   not believe   live   paint (x2)   travel   walk

Aelita Andre was once described as the youngest professional artist in the world. She ¹_____ since she was nine months old. In fact, she ²_____ before she ³_____ or talk. When she was two, an art gallery director saw her paintings and decided to exhibit them. When he found out how old she was, he ⁴_____ it.

Aelita's paintings have sold for thousands of dollars, and she ⁵_____ to see them in prestigious art galleries all over the world.

She usually leads a pretty normal life. She ⁶_____ the violin, is learning the drums, and would like to ⁷_____ forever!

Go to **Communication practice:** Student A page 161, Student B page 170

7 **A** Complete each sentence with two pieces of information about yourself.

1 I've never been able to _____ .
2 I hope I'll be able to _____ in ten years.
3 I'd love to be able to _____ in the future.
4 I was able to _____ when I was younger.

B In pairs, ask and answer questions about the sentences in 7A. Give more information.

A *What have you never been able to do?*
B *Well, I've never been able to sing very well. I love singing, but I sound awful!*

Personal Best   Make excuses for missing a class yesterday, a party today, and a doctor's appointment tomorrow.   63

7D Could you tell me where it is?

1 What do you prefer to do when you need directions to get somewhere? Why?

- use a folded map or street guide
- use a GPS or online map
- ask someone for directions

2 ▶ 7.13 Watch or listen to the first part of *Learning Curve* and answer the questions.

1 Where is Taylor going?
2 What is she going to do there?
3 How does she try to get directions there?

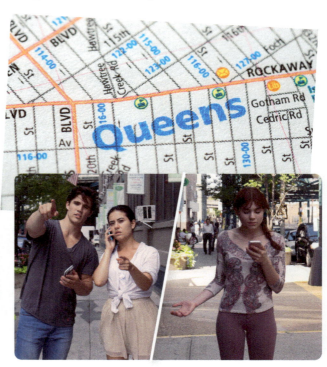

3 ▶ 7.13 Watch or listen again. Are the sentences true (T) or false (F)? Correct the false sentences.

1 Taylor is near a park. _____
2 She's on 23rd Street. _____
3 Ethan tells her to take 23rd Avenue and keep going straight past the park. _____
4 Penny tells her the movie theater is near the department store. _____

🔧 Conversation builder	**giving directions**
Describing the location	**Saying how to get there**
The ... is on the other side of the ...	Take/Go up 23rd Street. / Follow this road.
It's on the left/right.	Go straight ahead. / Keep going straight (until you get to/come to ...)
It's across from/next to/near a ...	Take a right / Turn right (at the traffic circle).
It's on Queen's Street.	Take the first right (after the traffic light).
It's ten minutes away on foot.	Go down/up/along/around/through/past the ...

4 Look at the map. Which icons represent the following places?

parking lot restaurant tourist information cell-phone store your house hospital gas station

5 Give your partner directions to one of the places on the map. Don't say which place it is. Your partner will follow your directions and tell you which place the directions were for.

6 ▶ 7.14   Watch or listen to the second part of the show. Answer the questions.

1 How many movie theaters are there in the neighborhood?   _____

2 What are they called?   _____

3 Which theater does Taylor want?   _____

4 Which road is it on?   _____

7 ▶ 7.14   How did Taylor ask the couple for directions? Complete the sentence. Watch or listen again and check.

> Excuse me. _____ to bother you, but do you know _____ the movie theater _____ ?

🔧 **Skill**   **asking for information**

When we ask for information, we try to sound polite. We can also politely ask for clarification or confirmation of the information.

- Begin with a polite phrase. *Excuse me. / Sorry to bother you, but ...*
- Use indirect questions, which sound more polite than direct ones.
  Do you know where the theater is? NOT ~~Do you know where is the theater?~~
  Could you tell me where the movie theater is? NOT ~~Could you tell me where is the movie theater?~~
- Use intonation to sound polite.
- Ask the person to clarify or confirm the information. *Sorry, did you say take a right? So, it's straight ahead and the first building on the left?*

8 ▶ 7.15   Read the Skill box. Listen to five people asking for information. Check (✔) the things that each speaker does and complete the chart.

speaker	begins with a polite phrase	uses an indirect question	uses polite intonation
1			
2			
3			
4			
5			

9 **A** ▶ 7.16   Make indirect questions. Listen, check, and repeat.

1 Where's the park?
  Could you tell me where _____ ?

2 Does this bus stop near the movie theater?
  Do you know if _____ ?

3 Is the movie theater downtown?
  Do you know if _____ ?

4 What's the name of this area?
  Could you tell me what _____ ?

5 Are there any vegetarian restaurants in this town?
  Do you know if _____ ?

B In pairs, ask and answer the indirect questions. Add a polite phrase to begin.

Go to Communication practice: Student A page 161, Student B page 165

10 **A** PREPARE   In pairs, choose a place in your town or city. Imagine you are there. Choose two other places and think about how to get there from your starting point.

B PRACTICE   Take turns asking for and giving directions to the places. Be polite when you ask for the information, and ask for clarification or confirmation if necessary.

C PERSONAL BEST   When you asked for information, did you sound polite? When you gave directions, were you clear? Can you make any improvements? Find another partner and ask and answer again.

Personal Best   Write directions from your local bus or train station to your place of work or study.

Sports and health

8A On the field, in the pool

1 ▶ 8.1 Listen to six sports commentators. Match the six sports places they mention with pictures a–f.

1 pool _____
2 circuit _____
3 court _____
4 field _____
5 track _____
6 rink _____

Go to Vocabulary practice:
sports, places, and equipment, page 148

Personal Best

2 **A** ▶ 8.5 Listen to a radio program about the unusual sports in the pictures. Complete the notes in the chart below.

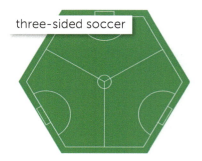
three-sided soccer

underwater hockey

bossaball

sport	three-sided soccer	underwater hockey	bossaball
Where is it played? What equipment is used?	On a hexagonal [1]_____ with three goals and a ball.	In a swimming pool, using a [3]_____ to push a "puck."	On a [5]_____ filled with air, with trampolines on each side of a [6]_____ .
How do you win?	By letting in fewer goals than the other [2]_____ .	The team with the most [4]_____ wins.	You [7]_____ points by hitting or kicking the ball over the net.

B Which of these sports would you like to try? Why?

3 ▶ 8.6 Complete the host's questions with the tag questions in the box. Listen and check.

isn't it   have you   can you   aren't you   didn't you   don't you

1 You're going to tell us about some unusual sports, _____ ?
2 It's pretty much like normal soccer, _____ ?
3 You actually played in a game this weekend, _____ ?
4 You can't swim very well, _____ ?
5 You have one last sport to talk about, _____ ?
6 You haven't played bossaball yet, _____ ?

4 **A** Look at the sentences in exercise 3 again. When do we use tag questions? Choose a or b.

a when we don't know the answer to the question

b when we already know the answer, but we're just checking

B Choose the best option to complete the rules. Then read the Grammar box.

1 When the statement is affirmative, the tag question is *affirmative / negative*.

2 When the statement is negative, the tag question is *affirmative / negative*.

3 We form tag questions with *an auxiliary + pronoun / a pronoun + auxiliary*.

> 📖 **Grammar** **tag questions**
>
> **Checking information:**
> She **plays** volleyball, **doesn't she**?
> We **saw** that movie last year, **didn't we**?
> Tom **doesn't eat** meat, **does he**?
>
> **Starting a conversation:**
> The bus **is** pretty late, **isn't it**?
> You **worked** in the bank, **didn't you**?
> The weather **isn't** very nice today, **is it**?

Go to Grammar practice: tag questions, page 126

5 **A** ▶8.8 **Pronunciation: intonation** Listen to the sentences. Does the intonation in the tag question go up (↗) or down (↘)?

1 We've been to this restaurant before, haven't we?

2 You can't come to the party tonight, can you?

3 Her last name's Henderson, isn't it?

4 Your sister doesn't have a car, does she?

5 You went to the gym this morning, didn't you?

6 They won't stay at her house all week, will they?

B ▶8.8 Listen again and repeat.

6 **A** Complete the sentences with a tag question.

1 It's about eight thirty now, _____ ?

2 The weather was awful yesterday, _____ ?

3 You didn't come to class last week, _____ ?

4 You aren't Canadian, _____ ?

5 It'll be a nice day tomorrow, _____ ?

6 You've done your homework, _____ ?

B In pairs, ask and answer the questions in 6A. If necessary, change the information in the sentences so you're checking information you already know.

A *It's about 7:15 now, isn't it?* **B** *Yes, it is.*

Go to Communication practice: Student A page 162, Student B page 171

7 **A** Ask and answer the questions in pairs. Try to remember your partner's answers, but don't write anything.

☐ Who's your favorite athlete?

☐ What sport does he/she play? Why do you like him/her?

☐ What sports do you play?

☐ When was the last time you played this sport/these sports?

☐ What sports could you play well when you were a child?

☐ Have you ever won a competition or race?

☐ What sports event would you like to watch live in a stadium?

B Look at the questions again. In pairs, check the answers using tag questions.

A *Your favorite athlete is Usain Bolt, isn't it?*

B *Yes, it is. You're right. / No, it isn't. It's Cristiano Ronaldo.*

 Personal Best Write six statements with tag questions to start a conversation with someone.

8B So many ways to get in shape

1 A Are the health and fitness facts and figures below true or false? Discuss your answers in pairs.

Health and fitness facts and figures

1 In a lot of countries, people spend millions on **healthy lifestyle** choices (gyms, fitness clubs, healthy food). They spend more than double the amount on fast food.

2 37% of people who pay for gym memberships to **get in shape** never use them.

3 About two thirds of adults are **overweight** or need to lose weight.

4 For a healthy, **balanced diet**, men need 2,000 calories a day, and women need 2,500.

B What do the words in **bold** mean? Compare your ideas in pairs.

Go to Vocabulary practice: health and fitness verb phrases, page 149

2 Answer the questions in pairs.

1 Do any of the facts in exercise 1A surprise you?
2 Do you have a healthy lifestyle?
3 What do you think the objects in the picture to the right are?
4 How do you think they help people get in shape?

3 ▶ 8.10 Watch or listen to the first part of *Learning Curve*. Check (✔) the facts which are mentioned.

a Ethan's app counts how many steps he takes every day. ☐
b The word *pedometer* means "foot measurer." ☐
c Pedometers were invented in Greece. ☐
d One in three people doesn't get any exercise at all. ☐
e People who work out with a partner are more motivated to get exercise. ☐
f The average cost of a gym is $700 a year. ☐

🔧 **Skill** | **understanding facts and figures**

When listening for detailed information, we often need to understand facts and figures accurately.

- Before you listen, find out what type of information you need to listen for. For example, is it a number, a person, a time, a place, etc?
- Use the general context to predict when you'll hear numbers, e.g., when talking about times, dates, distances, prices, and percentages.
- Recognize words that often follow numbers: currencies ($, £, €), percent, decimal points, and ways of describing statistics: *one in four people, one fifth of the population, the average, three times as many*.

---

4 ▶ 8.10 Read the Skill box. Watch or listen again and answer the questions.

1 How many extra steps do pedometer users take every day? _____
2 What percentage of people in the U.S. get enough physical activity? _____
3 How many miles do people walk if they take 10,000 steps a day? _____
4 What percentage of couples who exercise separately quit? _____
5 What percentage of couples who exercise together quit? _____

5 Discuss the questions in pairs. Give reasons for your answers.

1 Do you enjoy walking as a way to keep active?
2 Have you ever used a pedometer, or would you like to try one?
3 Is exercising with a friend or partner a good idea?

Bindi

Taylor

Joe

Louis

6 ▶ 8.11 Watch or listen to the second part of the show. Are the sentences true or false? Correct the false sentences.

1 Bindi does weightlifting once a week. _____
2 Taylor's client is training for the Ironman triathlon. _____
3 Ironman athletes swim 2.4 miles, cycle 112 miles and run 26 miles. _____
4 Half a marathon is 30 miles. _____
5 Joe has always been in good shape and healthy. _____
6 Joe and his wife took up ballroom dancing. _____
7 Neither Joe nor Louis go to the gym. _____
8 Louis doesn't get a lot of exercise. _____

7 Would you like to take up triathlon training, weightlifting, or ballroom dancing? Why / Why not? Discuss in pairs.

🎽 **Listening builder** | **intonation**

When listening to fast English, listen for phrases which help you follow units of meaning. In a phrase, the intonation usually falls towards the end.

There are so many ways to get in shape.

Some people play sports, while others eat a balanced diet and stay active.

8 **A** ▶ 8.12 Read the Listening builder. Listen to these sentences. How many phrases does the speaker use?

1 She's trained with me for three months and works very hard.
2 We take classes twice a week and go out dancing every Saturday night.
3 One study looked at married people who joined a gym together.
4 At the end of the day, people feel good when they meet their goals.

B ▶ 8.12 Listen again and pay attention to the intonation. Then practice saying the sentences.

9 In groups, discuss the following statement:

Our generation is a lot healthier than our parents and grandparents were at our age.

You could talk about the following things:

amount of exercise   diet   amount of stress   sleep   good or bad habits

Personal Best   Describe a healthy day you've had recently and an unhealthy one.

8C Is there an app for that?

1 A What apps do you have on your phone? What are they for? How often do you use them?

B Look at the three apps. What do you think each app does? How can they help you improve your health?

2 A Read the posts by Sophie, Tom, and Kate below. They ask their friend Rob, a fitness expert, for advice. What problems do they have? Choose the correct options.

1 Sophie *can't sleep at night / isn't sure how much sleep she needs*.
2 Tom *feels out of shape / wants to lose weight*.
3 Kate *is looking for a new job / is stressed out*.

B Which app do you think Rob recommends for each person? Read his replies and check.

 Sophie
I have to get up at 5 a.m. every day as I start work at 7. I don't go to bed till after midnight, so I'm only getting 5 hours of sleep a night. When I drive to work, I'm so sleepy! How do I know if I'm getting enough sleep? @RobDanes, you have a lot of health apps – can you recommend one for me?

 Rob
Check out *Sleep Friend*. It tells you when you should go to bed and get up. It also monitors sleep cycles, so it knows when you're in a light sleep or a deep sleep, and its alarm goes off when you're sleeping lightly. You should get more than 6 hours of sleep a night, though, and you can't drive when you're very tired!

 Tom
Rob, I didn't know you were such an expert! Got any suggestions for me? This morning I had to run for the bus, and I felt awful. I'm so out of shape. I really have to get more exercise, but I just don't have time to go to the gym or take fitness classes.

 Rob
Hi Tom! You don't have to go to the gym to get in shape. Try the *Workout for 7* app. It's really worked for me. You exercise really hard for 7 minutes, and it has the same effect as going running or working out at the gym. The app shows you exactly what to do.

 Kate
While you're giving everyone advice, Rob, can you give me some? I really need to chill out. I'm so anxious about my new job that I can't relax, and it's really worrying me. I've heard that meditation can help. Is there an app for that?

 Rob
Hey Kate! You shouldn't worry about it – we all get stressed. Just learn some meditation techniques that you can do at home regularly. Get the *iRelax* app. It shows you what to do, creates a meditation schedule, and reminds you when to do it. Good luck and let's get together soon.

3 A Are the sentences true (T) or false (F)? Correct the false sentences.

1 *Sleep Friend* wakes you up when you're in a deep sleep. _____
2 *Workout for 7* isn't as good as going running. _____
3 *iRelax* tells you when to meditate. _____

B Complete the sentences with the words in the box. Who said each sentence? Check your answers in the text.

> can't   have to (x2)   should   don't have to   shouldn't

1 I _____ get up at 5 a.m. every day.
2 You _____ get more than six hours of sleep.
3 You _____ drive when you're very tired!
4 I really _____ do more exercise.
5 You _____ go to the gym to get in shape.
6 You _____ worry about it.

4 Match the sentences in exercise 3B with functions a–f. Then read the Grammar box.

a It isn't necessary to do this. There isn't any obligation. _____
b I think it's a good idea to do this. _____
c It's prohibited or against the law to do this. _____
d I don't think it's a good idea to do this. _____
e It's necessary to do this. It's an external obligation. _____
f It's necessary to do this. It's a personal obligation. _____

📖 **Grammar**   **modals of obligation and advice**

Obligation:
We **have to** be at the airport at 2 p.m.
She **has to** remember to get Jo a birthday present.

No obligation:
I **don't have to** get up early. It's Sunday.

Prohibition:
You **can't** take photos in the museum.

Advice:
You **should** go to bed earlier.
You **shouldn't** swim after eating.

Go to Grammar practice: modals of obligation and advice, page 127

5 A ▶8.14 **Pronunciation:** sentence stress Listen to the sentences. Underline the stressed words or syllables.

1 She has to leave now.
2 You don't have to pay to enter.
3 I have to remember my keys this time!
4 You can't speak during the test.
5 They should get a cab.
6 You shouldn't eat so much cheese.

B ▶8.14 Listen again and repeat the sentences.

6 A ▶8.15 Listen to a radio program about rules and laws in different countries. Complete the sentences with the missing information and the correct form of *have to, can,* or *should*.

1 In some places in India, people studying to be teachers _____ take _____ classes, and soon police officers will _____ do the same.
2 In some Indian states, you _____ use your _____ while driving, even if it's a hands-free device.
3 In the U.S., you _____ talk too loudly on your cell phone. It can be considered _____ .
4 In Canada, you _____ wear a _____ when riding a motorcycle and a normal bicycle.
5 On the Internet, it says that in California you _____ ride your bike in a _____ !
6 In France, children _____ go to school on _____ , but they _____ go on Wednesday afternoons, or wear a uniform.

B Is it the same or different in your country? Discuss in pairs.

Go to Communication practice: Student A page 162, Student B page 171

7 In pairs, talk about …

• something you've had to get up really early for.
• something important you have to remember to do this month.
• something you'll have to do next year.
• something a relative or teacher often says you should or shouldn't do.
• something you can't do in high school/in college/at work.
• something you often had to do when you were younger.

Personal Best Write a message asking Rob for advice. Then write Rob's reply.

8D Sports in my country

1 Read the webpage and look at the pictures. Have you tried any of these sports, seen them live, or watched them on TV? Discuss in pairs.

International *SPORTS* Organization

Which sports are popular in your country? Which sports activities would you recommend to a visitor to your country?
Write a report for ISO members about sports in your country, and we will post it on this webpage.

Jude, U.S.

 baseball
 football
 basketball

POSTED: 12 May
SEE *MORE* ...

David, Argentina

 soccer
 surfing
 volleyball

POSTED: 18 May
SEE *MORE* ...

Maarit, Finland

 ice-swimming
 hockey
 pesäpallo

POSTED: 25 May
SEE *MORE* ...

2 A Read the first paragraph of a report from the website. Who wrote the report: Jude, David, or Maarit?

Sports in my country

1 _____

Sports are a very popular leisure activity in my country, and there are fantastic facilities in most towns and cities. Finland has a very cold climate, though, and in winter, parts of the country are covered with snow for six months. This means that people enjoy doing different sports activities in different seasons.

2 _____

Cross-country skiing is an extremely popular sport here. As there are very few mountains in Finland, people ski on flat land through the country's forests. It is a great way to stay in shape and enjoy the country's natural beauty. Ice skating and hockey are popular as well as skiing. Moreover, hockey, ski jumping, and snowboarding are popular spectator sports.

3 _____

A lot of Finns enjoy swimming in indoor and outdoor pools, in the sea, or in the country's lakes. In addition to this, thousands of people regularly go ice-swimming.

They go to frozen lakes where they cut holes in the ice and jump in the water. I would recommend going ice-swimming after a visit to a hot sauna, which is another national tradition.

4 _____

It is easy to play any of the world's most popular sports here. There are tennis courts and soccer fields everywhere, and basketball has recently become very popular. In addition, if you are interested in discovering Finnish sports, I suggest trying pesäpallo. This is a fast-moving bat-and-ball sport that is similar to baseball and is usually played in the warmer summer months.

5 _____

Sports are a big part of life in Finland. This is one reason why the country produces many world champions, like Formula One auto-racing driver Mika Häkkinen. It is possible to practice any major sport here, but while you are visiting us, remember to try out our local sports and traditional activities as well.

B Read the whole report. Do you think it's interesting and easy to follow? Discuss in pairs.

🔧 **Skill** **writing a report**

Make your report interesting and easy for the reader to follow.
- Organize the content of your report into sections with one main topic in each section. A section can contain one or more paragraphs.
- Use headings for each section of your report.
- Include relevant factual information, and make some suggestions or recommendations for the reader, e.g. *I suggest* + *-ing*, *I would recommend* + *-ing*, *remember to* + base form.
- Reports are usually fairly formal, so avoid using informal language.

3 A Read the Skill box. Match headings a–e with sections 1–5 in the report.

a Our success at sports _____
b National and international sports _____
c Sports and climate in my country _____
d Winter sports _____
e Water sports _____

B What recommendations does the writer make? Match sentence parts 1–3 with a–c to make complete sentences. Then check your answers in the text.

1 I would recommend
2 If you are interested in discovering Finnish sports, I suggest
3 While you are visiting us, remember

a trying pesäpallo.
b to try out our local sports and traditional activities.
c going ice-swimming.

🧩 **Text builder** **adding information**

We can use these phrases to add information to a sentence or paragraph:

as well	*There is a national tournament every year, and there are several regional competitions, **as well**.*
as well as	*Swimming, bicycling, and walking are all popular with adults, **as well as** children.*
In addition (to this)	***In addition to** road cycling, track cycling is popular as a spectator sport.*
	*We have had great international success in soccer in recent years. **In addition**, our national basketball team has won the World Championship twice.*

Look! We can use *moreover* instead of *in addition* in more formal writing:
*Sports keep you in shape. **Moreover**, they are a good way to meet people.*

4 Read the Text builder. Look at the report again and answer the questions.
1 Find one example of each *as well* phrase in Maarit's report.
2 What does *this* refer to in the *In addition to this* phrase?

5 Write complete sentences with the prompts and the phrases in **bold**.
1 many parks / public tennis courts / table tennis tables
as well as
2 Formula One / a popular spectator sport / motorcycle racing / becoming more popular
in addition
3 our beaches / perfect for inexperienced surfers / advanced surfers
as well
4 this traditional game / great fun / it / a great way to stay in shape
moreover
5 our soccer team / won the World Cup / our baseball team / very successful
in addition to this

6 A PREPARE Think about which sports are popular in your country and what recommendations you would make for a visitor. Plan four or five section headings.

B PRACTICE Use the Skill box to help you write a report on sports in your country. Include relevant information under each section heading.

C PERSONAL BEST Choose two or three sections from your report. Read them aloud to your partner, but don't read the section heading. Can your partner guess the headings for each section?

Personal Best Think of a sports activity in your local area that people can do for free. Add an extra section to your report.

Grammar

1 Choose the correct options to complete the sentences.

1 The play *Romeo and Juliet* _____ by Shakespeare.
   a wrote   b was written   c be written

2 I would like to _____ play the guitar like you.
   a can   b could   c be able to

3 Stephen's been working there for years, _____ ?
   a is he   b isn't he   c hasn't he

4 You _____ take a taxi to the airport. I can drive you.
   a don't have to   b have to   c couldn't

5 The new James Bond movie _____ in Mexico.
   a is going to filmed   b is going to be filmed
   c is going to be film

6 _____ speak to Mike or Alan this week?
   a Have you able to   b Have you been able to
   c Have you could

7 It won't rain this afternoon, _____ ?
   a won't it   b it won't   c will it

8 You _____ use your cell phone while you're driving.
   It's against the law.
   a can't   b don't have to   c have to

2 Use the structures in parentheses to complete the sentences so they mean the same as the first sentence.

1 I think you passed the test. Am I right? (tag question)
   You passed the test, _____ ?

2 I hope I can go up the Empire State Building when I visit New York. (modal of possibility)
   I hope I'll _____ up the Empire State Building when I visit New York.

3 George Lucas directed the first *Star Wars* movie. (passive)
   The first *Star Wars* movie _____ George Lucas.

4 It's not necessary to pay to use expressway in the UK. (modal of obligation)
   You _____ to use expressways in the UK.

5 The new factory will make over 500,000 cars a year. (passive)
   Over 500,000 cars a year _____ at the new factory.

6 I couldn't drive until I was 22 years old. (modal of ability)
   I wasn't _____ until I was 22 years old.

7 I don't think you'll be able to come to my wedding. Is that true? (tag question)
   You won't be able to come to my wedding, _____ ?

8 It's not a good idea to go swimming just after lunch. (modal of advice)
   You _____ just after lunch.

3 Choose the correct options to complete the text.

Could you be a mentor?

Developing your new career or business ¹*can / can't* be easier with a mentor – someone with experience in the same industry who can help and encourage you. One famous mentor was Steve Jobs, who ²*was guided by / guided* Mark Zuckerberg in the early days of Facebook. We talk to Laura and Rob about their experience of mentoring.

Laura, what does the role of mentor involve?

My role is to encourage Rob and give him advice, like "You ³*should / can* do some more market research."

But you can't make decisions for him, ⁴*can / can't* you?

No. Rob ⁵*has / doesn't have* to make his own decisions. A good mentor ⁶*can / has to* believe in the person's ability to develop.

Rob, you had a difficult time before you met Laura, ⁷*hadn't / didn't* you?

Yes. I had a lot of knowledge about the industry, but no experience. Laura's given me a lot of practical advice, which has helped build my confidence. I got a promotion yesterday, and it's great to know I ⁸*could / 'll be able to* talk to her about any issues that come up in my new role.

Vocabulary

1 Circle the word that is different. Explain your answer.

1	documentary	thriller
	director	action movie
2	pool	field
	racket	court
3	track and field	diving
	track	auto racing
4	game show	channel
	sitcom	soap opera
5	tracks	playlist
	hits	cast
6	have a balanced diet	get a good night's sleep
	get exercise	have bad habits
7	net	bat
	stick	rink

2 Match the words in the box with definitions 1–10.

> plot   court   be in shape   sequel   script   soundtrack
> romantic comedy   audience   episode   cartoon

1   have good physical health because of
     exercise   _____
2   the music that is played during a movie   _____
3   the story of a movie or book   _____
4   a funny movie about love   _____
5   the place where you play ball games   _____
6   a part of a TV series   _____
7   a TV show with characters that are
     drawn   _____
8   a movie that continues the story of a previous
     movie   _____
9   the people who watch a TV show live in the
     studio   _____
10 the written form of a movie   _____

3 Complete the sentences with the words in the box.

> live   set in   scene   hits   get stressed
> horror   musicals   album

1   I don't usually enjoy _____ because I don't like it
     when the story is told through songs.
2   Have you ever seen your favorite singer _____ in
     concert?
3   The movie *Titanic* stars Leonardo DiCaprio and is
     _____ 1912.
4   It's not healthy to _____ so often.
5   I think this is the band's best _____ . It has lots of their
     biggest _____ on it.
6   That's the most terrifying _____ movie I've ever seen!
7   My favorite _____ in the movie is the car chase
     through Moscow.

4 Put the words in the box in the correct columns.

> series   shot   net   playlist   ice skating   subtitles
> on tour   ads   ball   talk show   band   the news
> animation   circuit   goal   special effects

movies	TV

sports	music

Personal Best

Lesson 7A
Name four movies you've seen and say what types of movies they are.

Lesson 8A
Name three sports places and three pieces of sports equipment.

Lesson 7A
Describe a movie in four sentences that use the passive.

Lesson 8A
Write three questions about your classmates using tag questions.

Lesson 7B
Write two sentences. In the second sentence, use *this* or *that* to refer to something in the first sentence.

Lesson 8B
Describe a healthy lifestyle using at least four verb phrases.

Lesson 7C
Name four TV shows you dislike and say what types of shows they are.

Lesson 8C
Write two sentences giving advice to a friend, using *should* and *shouldn't*.

Lesson 7C
Write three sentences about a friend using *be able to* in different forms.

Lesson 8C
Write three sentences about your English class using *have to*, *don't have to*, and *can't*.

Lesson 7D
Say three expressions you can use when you give directions.

Lesson 8D
Add some information to your sentence with *have to* (8C), using *as well as*.

LANGUAGE | uses of *like* ■ food and cooking

9A Chefs at home

1 Look at the pictures. Find the words for each item of food in the text.

a _____ b _____ c _____ d _____ e _____ f _____ g _____

2 Read the text. Would you like to try any of the dishes? Which one(s)?

TOP CHEFS
...AT HOME

They're famous around the world for the delicious food in their restaurants. But what do the world's top chefs like to cook for themselves at the end of a long day or week at work?

Mitsuharu Tsumura (Lima)

Mitsuharu cooks sukiyaki for his family on Sunday. It's a meat dish, usually thinly sliced beef, which is slowly cooked at the table with vegetables, **soy sauce**, and sugar. The meat is then dipped in a small bowl of egg.

Alain Allegretti (New York)

Alain loves cooking pasta at the end of a long day when he wants something quick, easy, and delicious. He suggests having it with **garlic** and **olive oil**, or with tomatoes and herbs.

Angela Hartnett (London)

When Angela is in a hurry, she makes canned tuna on **toast** with mayonnaise. For a simple yet special treat, her favorite dish is scrambled eggs on toast, which she recommends cooking very slowly.

Daniel Boulud (New York)

Daniel makes *salade meridionale* at home when he wants to relax. It's a salad with **shellfish**, **avocado**, eggplant, olives, peppers, **zucchini**, and other vegetables, with pesto and lemon.

Personal Best

Go to Vocabulary practice: food and cooking, page 150

3 A ▶9.4 Listen to three people talking about a dish they like. Put the dishes in the order they are mentioned from 1–3.

a ☐

b ☐

c ☐

B ▶ 9.4 Match questions 1–3 with replies a–g. Listen again and check your answers.

1 What do you like to eat at the end of a long day? _____ _____ _____
2 What's it like? _____ _____ _____
3 Would you like to try it? _____

a It's like spaghetti, but thicker.
b It's delicious.
c Soup with meatballs.
d No, thanks. I've already eaten!

e This! It's called *poutine*.
f Really tasty.
g Udon noodles.

4 Underline four phrases with *like* in exercise 3B. Match them with the meanings of *like* (a–d) below. Then read the Grammar box.

a asking about a preference _____
b saying that something is similar _____
c asking for a description of something _____
d making a polite offer _____

📖 **Grammar** **uses of *like***

Talking about preferences:
*What do you **like** doing on Sundays?*
*I **like** going to the movies.*

Talking about similarity:
*He's **like** his father – very lazy!*
*She **looks like** her mother.*

Asking for a description:
*What's the weather **like**?*
*What **was** the party **like**?*

Making a polite offer or request:
***Would** you **like** a cup of coffee?*
*I'**d like** the chicken salad, please.*

Look! We also use ***would like*** for something you want to do or have:
*I'**d like** to go home now.   I'**d** really **like** a motorcycle.*

Personal Best

Go to Grammar practice: uses of *like*, page 128

5 **A** ▶ 9.6 **Pronunciation:** /dʒ/ sound *Did you* and *would you* can be pronounced with a /dʒ/ sound (like *job*). Listen to the questions. When do you hear /dʒ/?

1 Would you like some tea?
2 What would you like for dinner?
3 Did you like the shellfish?
4 What did you eat for breakfast?

B ▶ 9.6 Listen again and repeat. In pairs, ask and answer the questions.

6 **A** Complete the conversation with the correct form of *like*.

A ¹_____ food from other countries?
B Yes, I do. I really ²_____ Thai and Japanese food. Actually, I make it for my roommates. The flavors are amazing.
A ³_____ the last dish you made?
B Yes, they did! I made sashimi. It ⁴_____ sushi, but without rice. I served it with soy sauce and wasabi.
A What ⁵_____ ?
B It was delicious – really fresh and tasty, and the wasabi was really hot.
A Mmmm, I ⁶_____ to try that! Tell me, ⁷_____ to work as a chef?
B Yes, I'd love to.

B In pairs, practice the conversation. Change the replies so they are true for you.

Go to Communication practice: Student A page 162, Student B page 171

7 Discuss the questions in pairs.

1 What do you like to cook or eat at the end of a long day? And at the end of the week?
2 Are you a good cook? Which dishes would you like to learn to make?
3 What was the first meal you cooked? What did it taste like?
4 What's your favorite dish for a special occasion? What's it like?
5 Have you ever eaten an unusual food or dish? What was it like?

 Personal Best   Write a short conversation about food. Use *like* in at least four different ways.

9B Chocolate – the world's favorite superfood

1 What do you think a *superfood* is? Read the first paragraph of the text on page 79 and check your answer.

2 Read the whole text quickly. Why is chocolate a superfood? Which five benefits are mentioned?

> ### 🔧 Skill   reading for detail
>
> **When answering multiple-choice questions, you often have to look for detailed information in a text.**
> - First, read the text quickly. Then read the questions and underline the key words.
> - Scan the text and find the part that contains the information you need. Read that part in detail.
> - If a word from the answer options appears in the text, it doesn't mean that option is the correct answer. Read the sentence carefully to make sure the meaning of the option is the same as in the text.

3 Read the Skill box. Then read the text again and choose the correct answers.

1 The author says that superfoods
   a are exciting.   **b** are unexciting.   **c** are unexciting, except for chocolate.

2 Where does cacao come from?
   a Panama   **b** Central America   **c** Germany

3 Why did the Kuna people have low blood pressure?
   a They drank tea.   **b** They were healthy.   **c** They drank cacao.

4 Which kind of chocolate has the most health benefits?
   a dark chocolate   **b** milk chocolate   **c** white chocolate

5 Which benefit does the author say is the most unusual?
   a Chocolate protects us from illness.
   b Chocolate makes us feel like we're in love.
   c Chocolate increases our intelligence.

6 What does the author warn the reader about? Choose two answers.
   a Chocolate isn't as healthy nowadays as it used to be.
   b Food with a high fat content can cause heart disease.
   c It's important to know who paid for the studies about chocolate and health.

> ### 🧩 Text builder   substitution: *one, ones*
>
> **To avoid repeating a noun from earlier in the sentence or in a previous sentence, we can substitute the word *one* (singular) or *ones* (plural):**
> *Foods that have received this label have been unexciting **ones** like spinach, garlic, or salmon.*
> *This creates the same **feeling** as the **one** you get when you fall in love.*

4 Read the Text builder. Underline the eight examples of *one* or *ones* in the text. Which four are used to avoid repeating a noun? Which nouns are they substituting?

5 Read the sentences. Underline the words that *one* or *ones* replace.

1 My train was delayed when I got to the station. The next one was an hour later, so I had to wait.
2 I was offered two free apps when I bought my phone. The ones I chose were both games.
3 There are lots of great restaurants all over the city, but the best ones are down by the harbor.
4 Every student was given the same math problem, but I was the only one who could solve it.
5 We serve lots of dishes in my restaurant, but the most popular ones are red curry and lasagna.

6 In pairs, discuss the questions.

1 Is there any food that is a "guilty pleasure" for you?
2 Have you heard of any other superfoods? Do you eat them?
3 Do you believe the reports about the health benefits of superfoods?

Chocolate – the superfood!

It's official! Chocolate is good for you! A team of researchers at the German Institute of Human Nutrition have discovered that there are many health benefits of eating chocolate every day. In fact, it's so good for you that it's being labeled the latest "superfood." Up to now, foods that have received this label have been unexciting ones like spinach, garlic, or salmon. Thankfully, now that chocolate has joined that elite group, we can all relax. That chocolate bar in your desk at lunchtime is no longer a guilty pleasure – it's a superfood.

Like many natural products, people have known for centuries that chocolate was a good thing, especially in Central America where cacao originated. The Aztec emperor Montezuma was particularly partial to it, drinking an estimated 50 cups a day (as an emperor with the power of life and death over his people, clearly nobody was brave enough to tell him that he couldn't have another one). Among the Kuna people of Panama, cacao was drunk like tea, and consequently, they had very low blood pressure.

There are many health benefits to eating chocolate on a regular basis. It's packed with minerals, especially ones such as selenium and zinc, which help fight disease. Chocolate is also an excellent source of flavanols, chemicals that lower your blood pressure and help keep your brain healthy, although neither milk nor white chocolate contain as high a percentage of these beneficial properties as dark chocolate does.

In addition to improving your physical health, chocolate makes you feel better, too. Researchers have discovered that eating chocolate releases a chemical in the brain that makes your heart beat more quickly. This creates the same feeling as the one you get when you fall in love. Perhaps most surprising of all, though, is the discovery that chocolate makes you smarter. One study found that countries where people eat the most chocolate also have the most Nobel Prizes. One example is Switzerland, home to Albert Einstein, where people eat an average of 9.5 kilos of chocolate a year!

Despite the evidence, some health experts remain critical of our love for chocolate. Unlike the Aztecs, people today rarely consume chocolate in its pure form. Instead, modern chocolate is often combined with milk and sugar, increasing its fat content. This means that professionals advise that chocolate should be consumed in moderation and only as part of a healthy diet.

There is one further warning. Some critics have taken a critical look at the "chocolate is good" news stories. They point out that some of the research "proving" the health benefits of chocolate was funded by the chocolate industry, so I recommend that you keep this in mind. Despite these criticisms, there's no doubt that chocolate makes you feel good. So, forget spinach, blueberries, and all the others – there's only one superfood you need, and it's **chocolate, chocolate, CHOCOLATE!**

 Personal Best   Write a paragraph about a healthy item of food.

9C Eating out

1 Look at the webpage below. What is unusual about Nadia's Place? Do you think a restaurant like this is a good idea?

Nadia's Place café and restaurant

Come and try the place everyone's talking about! At **Nadia's Place**, we have no prices. Instead, we have an honesty payment system. You decide how much you want to pay, depending on the quality of the food, atmosphere, and service. Pop in for coffee and cake, or join us for lunch or dinner.

Menu

1 _____
Mushroom soup with homemade bread
Asparagus and boiled egg
Smoked salmon with cream cheese

2 _____
Chickpea, lime, and coconut curry
Grilled steak with black pepper sauce
Lemon roast chicken

3 _____
Mixed salad
French fries or baked potatoes
Onion rings

4 _____
Chocolate brownie
Fried bananas with melted chocolate
Strawberry cheesecake

2 Complete blanks 1–4 in the menu with the words in the box.

> Desserts   Main courses   Side dishes   Appetizers

Go to Vocabulary practice: eating out, page 151

3 Discuss the questions in pairs.
1 Think about the last time you ate out. What was the food, atmosphere, and service like?
2 What food would you order at Nadia's Place?

4 ▶ 9.9 Listen to an interview with Nadia. Order the topics she talks about from 1–5.
a ☐ future plans
b ☐ reactions to honesty payment
c ☐ how successful the business is
d ☐ the atmosphere
e ☐ reasons for opening Nadia's Place

5 A ▶ 9.10 Complete the sentences with the correct form of the verb in parentheses. Then listen and check.
1 Tell us why you decided _____ (open) a café-restaurant with no prices.
2 I opened this place _____ (do) something different.
3 _____ (eat) here is like having lunch at a friend's house.
4 It's a real community, and it's easy _____ (meet) new people.
5 I love _____ (come) to work each and every day!
6 In fact, we're thinking about _____ (open) a second café in an old theater.

B Match the sentences in 5A with rules a–f. Then read the Grammar box.

We use the *-ing* form:
a after some verbs, e.g., *like, love, enjoy, finish*. _____
b after prepositions. _____
c when a verb is the subject of the sentence. _____

We use the infinitive with *to*:
d after some verbs, e.g., *afford, decide, want*. _____
e after adjectives. _____
f to give a reason. _____

Personal Best

Grammar   -ing forms and infinitives

-ing forms:
- after some verbs:
*As soon as he **finished eating**, he asked for the check.*
- after prepositions:
*I'm not very good **at remembering** people's names.*
- when a verb is the subject of the sentence:
***Drinking** too much coffee is bad for you.*

Infinitives:
- after some verbs:
*We **decided to leave** a big tip as the service was excellent.*
- after adjectives:
*It's **nice to try** something different when you eat out.*
- to give a reason:
*I searched online **to find** a place that sells leather bags.*

Go to Grammar practice: -ing forms and infinitives, page 129

6 A ▶ 9.12 **Pronunciation:** *-ing* -ing is pronounced with an /ɪŋ/ sound (like *sing*), but in informal conversation, it is sometimes pronounced /ɪn/ (like *bin*). Listen to the sentences. When do you hear /ɪn/?

1 I'm not very good at doing the dishes.
2 Making birthday cakes is great fun.
3 I'm not very interested in reading books.
4 I don't mind driving if you're too tired.
5 He's interested in learning Arabic.
6 Choosing a dessert is always difficult!

B ▶ 9.12 Listen again and repeat the sentences.

7 Choose the correct options to complete the text.

I'd heard about an interesting new café in town, so yesterday, a friend and I went there ¹*to try / trying* it. It's a really unusual place: the food and drink is free, but you pay for each minute you're there. Lots of people enjoy ²*to spend / spending* time in a café, but not everyone can afford ³*to buy / buying* lots of food and drink, so this café is a nice alternative.

Everyone has to make his or her own drinks and snacks and do the dishes, so it's a bit like ⁴*to be / being* at home. We made ourselves some toast and coffee. ⁵*To use / Using* the coffee machine was a bit challenging, but we managed it in the end!

At first, my friend found it hard ⁶*to relax / relaxing* completely as she was watching the clock and counting every minute, but the atmosphere was friendly, and ⁷*to have / having* the freedom to make our own drinks and snacks was great. We're definitely going back, and my friend has promised ⁸*to not / not to* worry about the clock next time!

Go to Communication practice: Student A page 163, Student B page 171

8 A Work in pairs. Complete the sentences with the correct form of the verbs in parentheses.

1 What kinds of restaurants do you like _____ to? Why? (go)
2 Is it easy _____ a table at your favorite restaurant on the weekend? (reserve)
3 Have you ever used an app _____ takeout for delivery? What was it like? (order)
4 Have you ever refused _____ something in a restaurant? Why? What happened? (eat)
5 _____ in a restaurants as a chef or waiter is very hard. Do you agree? (work)
6 Do you get excited about _____ new dishes, or do you prefer _____ ones you've had before? (try, eat)
7 Do you think it's important _____ about where the food we eat comes from? (think)
8 What's the next special occasion in your life? What will you do _____ it? (celebrate)

B Ask and answer the questions in 8A in pairs.

Personal Best   Write a paragraph about your favorite place to have lunch.

Learning Curve

9D Why don't you try the curry?

1 A Look at the dictionary definition below. Then do the quiz.

> **foodie** *noun (informal)* a person with a particular interest in different types of good food and who enjoys new food experiences as a hobby.

Are you a **foodie**?

1	When you eat out, you always want to discuss what you're eating.	YES	NO
2	You can identify the different ingredients in a new dish.	YES	NO
3	You always have an opinion about every dish that you order.	YES	NO
4	You always want to try a new restaurant to see what the chef does.	YES	NO
5	You want to try all kinds of national and international cooking.	YES	NO
6	You care about the quality of the ingredients in what you eat.	YES	NO

B In pairs, discuss your answers. Are you a foodie?

2 ▶ **9.13** Watch or listen to the first part of *Learning Curve*. Check (✔) the things that are true about Jack.

1 He's an assistant chef. ☐
2 He's "Employee of the month." ☐
3 He writes a blog about food. ☐
4 He reviews restaurants for a magazine. ☐

3 ▶ **9.13** Complete Simon and Jack's sentences with the words in the box. Watch or listen again and check.

> suggest   could   would   what   honest   about   rather   wondering

Simon:
- ¹_____ you like to try some?
- How ²_____ that one?
- To be ³_____, I'd ⁴_____ have the aubergine (eggplant).

Jack:
- So, ⁵_____ about the courgette (zucchini)?
- I ⁶_____ you try this chicken dish.
- I was ⁷_____ if we ⁸_____ have dessert now.

🧩 Conversation builder   making and responding to suggestions

Making suggestions	Responding positively to suggestions	Responding negatively to suggestions
Should we ...?		
Would you like to ...?	Yes, let's.	Well, I'm not sure. I think I'd prefer ...
I suggest you/we ...		
I was wondering if we could ...	Of course.	To be honest, I'd rather ....
Why don't you/we ...?	That sounds great.	I won't, if that's OK.
How/What about ...?	Sure.	Can't we ... instead?
Have you thought about/of ...?	Great idea!	

---

4 A Read the Conversation builder. In pairs, take turns reading sentences 1–5 and responding.

1 Should we go out for dinner tonight?
2 I was wondering if we could try the new Thai restaurant.
3 I suggest we get there at nine thirty.
4 Can't we get there a bit earlier, instead? How about eight thirty?
5 Why don't we ask some friends to join us?

B In pairs, make your own suggestions about eating out together and respond.

5 ▶ 9.14 Watch or listen to the second part of the show. Answer the questions.

1 Which two dishes do they rate?
2 Do they agree or disagree about their ratings?

6 ▶ 9.14 Who says these sentences, Jack, Kate, or Simon? Watch or listen again and check.

1 What do you think of the courgette?   _____
2 I love it. Delicious.   _____
3 Only one star? Oh, come on, Simon.   _____
4 It's delicious. Simon?   _____
5 OK, then. Two stars!   _____
6 I agree, but I say two stars because I thought it was very dry.   _____
7 We'll have to agree to disagree!   _____

🔧 **Skill** **making a group decision**

When we want to make a group decision, we can:
• invite others to give their opinions and give our own.
• try to persuade others to change their minds, or be persuaded to change our own mind!
• accept that not everyone might agree in the end.

7 Look at exercise 6 again. Put sentences 1–7 into the correct column in the chart.

asking for and giving opinions	persuading others and changing your mind	agreeing or disagreeing

8 **A** Order sentences a–f to make a conversation.

a ☐ **Ben**   OK, then! They have some good dishes. But some of the others are boring.
b ☐ **Carl**   Oh, come on! Their fish and seafood dishes are fantastic!
c ☐ **Alice** What do you think about the food at the Western Hotel?
d ☐ **Carl**   I think we'll have to agree to disagree!
e ☐ **Ben**   I think it's a bit boring.
f ☐ **Alice** I agree with Carl. I had some wonderful seafood there a couple of weeks ago.

B ▶ 9.15 Listen and check. Practice the conversation in groups of three.

Go to Communication practice: Student A page 163, Student B page 172

9 **A** PREPARE You are planning a special meal with some friends. In groups, think of suggestions for where to eat and what type of food to have. Use the ideas in the pictures or your own.

B PRACTICE In your groups, practice the conversation. Make suggestions, respond, and make a group decision if possible.

C PERSONAL BEST Identify one part of the conversation that you could improve and change it. Practice the conversation again. Do the other students in your group think it's improved?

Personal Best Make a list of three restaurants in your town or area. Give each one 1–5 stars and the reason for your opinion.

Right and wrong

| LANGUAGE | reported speech ■ crime |

10A Smooth criminals?

1 A Read the four headlines. Which are about a crime? Which are about a punishment?

1 Thief sent to **prison** for five years

3 $10,000 stolen in bank **robbery**

2 Sixth **burglary** this week on Elm St.

4 Man gets huge **fine** for driving too fast

B Match the words in **bold** in 1A with definitions a–d.

a money you pay as punishment _____
b stealing from a store or a bank _____
c a place where criminals are sent _____
d entering a home and stealing _____

Go to Vocabulary practice: crime, page 152

2 Ask and answer the questions in pairs.

1 Is there a lot of crime where you live?
2 What crime stories have been in the news recently?

3 Look at the picture in the text. What is on the men's faces? Read the text and check your answers.

Men attempt burglary with "worst disguise ever"

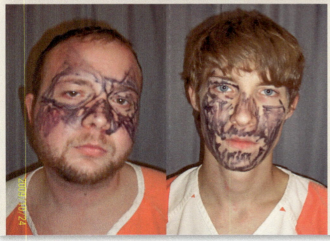

Two men have been arrested in Carroll, Iowa and charged with attempted burglary. Matthew McNelly, 23, and Joey Miller, 20, were caught after neighbors called 911 and said that two men were trying to break into an apartment. When police officers arrived at the apartment building, they asked witnesses what the men looked like. They said the men were wearing masks and black sweatshirts, and another witness told police they had driven away in a white car.

But when police spotted the white car shortly after and stopped it, they were amazed by what they saw. Instead of wearing real masks, the two burglars had drawn masks and beards on their faces with permanent black marker pen to hide their identities. One witness told reporters it was the worst disguise ever. It seems that, ironically, the "masks" were inspired by fictional crime-fighting superhero, Batman.

A legal expert said the pair would appear in court in a few weeks with their lawyers, and they would be charged with attempted burglary. Reporters asked the lawyers if they could comment on the case, but they did not respond.

4 A Who said these things? Write W (witness/es), P (police), R (reporters) or LE (legal expert).

1 "What **do** the men **look** like?" _____
2 "The men **are wearing** masks." _____
3 "They **drove** away." _____
4 "The pair **will appear** in court." _____
5 "**Can** you **comment**?" _____

B How are the sentences in 4A reported? Complete 1–5 below. Check your answers in the text.

1 They _____ witnesses _____ the men **looked** like.
2 They _____ the men **were wearing** masks.
3 Another witness _____ police they **had driven** away.
4 A legal expert _____ the pair **would appear** in court.
5 Reporters _____ the lawyers _____ they **could comment**.

5 Look at the sentences in exercises 4A and 4B and answer the questions. Then read the Grammar box.

1 How do the tenses and forms change from direct speech (4A) to reported speech (4B)?

1 simple present	→ _____	4 future with *will* → _____
2 present continuous	→ _____	5 *can* → _____
3 simple past	→ _____	

2 Look again at exercise 4A. Which sentence is a *yes/no* question? Which is a *wh-* question? How do we report these two types of questions?

📖 Grammar | reported speech

Direct statements: | **Reported statements:**
"*I'm feeling* tired." → | *She said (that) she **was feeling** tired.*
"*I **can't** swim.*" → | *Sam told us (that) he **couldn't** swim.*
"*It **won't** rain.*" → | *He said (that) it **wouldn't** rain.*

Direct questions: | **Reported questions:**
"***Do** you **like** sushi?*" → | *She asked me **if I liked** sushi.*
"***Where did** you **go**?*" → | *He asked me **where I had gone**.*

Look! In reported questions, we don't use a question form:
*She asked me **if I liked** sushi.* NOT ~~She asked me if did I like~~

Personal Best

Go to Grammar practice: reported speech, page 130

6 A ▶ 10.5 **Pronunciation: sentence stress** Listen to the sentences. Do we stress *if* and *that*? Do we stress *wh-* words?

1 They asked if I could help.
2 She asked if it would snow.
3 She told me that she'd passed!

4 I asked her why she'd left.
5 He asked me when I'd come.
6 I asked her where you'd gone.

B ▶ 10.5 Listen again and repeat.

7 A Who said these sentences and questions? Match 1–8 with the people in the box.

salesclerk   weather forecaster   boss   teacher   dentist   neighbor   criminal   police officer

1 "You'll have to work on the weekend." _____
2 "I didn't do it!" _____
3 "This won't hurt at all." _____
4 "Why haven't you done the homework?" _____
5 "Where were you at 9 p.m. on Friday?" _____
6 "Do you want to pay by credit card?" _____
7 "Can you turn the music down?" _____
8 "There may be storms this weekend." _____

B Change 1–8 in 7A into reported speech.

My boss told me …

Go to Communication practice: Student A page 163, Student B page 172

8 A In pairs, ask and answer four of the questions.

1 What's your favorite English word?
2 Which ad on TV do you hate? Why do you hate this ad?
3 Are you going to go out on Friday night?

4 Have you ever paid a fine?
5 What did you do last night?
6 Can you touch your toes?
7 Will you move in the next two years?

B In different pairs, discuss which questions you were asked and what you replied.

He asked me what my favorite English word was. I told him it was "enough."

Personal Best | Write four things your teacher has said in class today using reported speech. |

10B Emergency!

1 Discuss the questions below in pairs.

1 What different kinds of emergency services are there?
2 How do you contact the different emergency services in your country?
3 Do you know any emergency service numbers in other countries?
4 The police are there to protect, inform, and educate. Do you agree with this statement?

2 Complete the rewritten statement from exercise 1.

The police are there to provide _____ , _____ , and _____ .

Go to Vocabulary practice: making nouns from verbs, page 149

3 ▶ **10.7** Watch or listen to the first part of *Learning Curve* and answer the questions.

1 Which two countries are mentioned?
2 What are the emergency phone numbers in these countries?
3 What nationality is Liz Francis?
4 Where did she go on vacation?

> **🔧 Skill** listening in detail
>
> **It's often important to understand detailed information at a phrase and sentence level, and understand how the details relate to each other.**
> • Read the questions and answer options carefully.
> • Identify the key words in the questions and answer options.
> • When listening, focus on the whole message, and not on individual words and phrases.
> • Don't choose an option based on hearing one word or phrase that appears in that option.

4 **A** ▶ **10.7** Read the Skill box and underline the key words in the questions and answer options below. Watch or listen again and choose the correct options to answer the questions.

1 What was the emergency situation?
  a Liz needed an ambulance as she'd injured her foot.
  b Liz needed help to escape a dangerous situation.
  c Liz saw someone fall off a cliff into the ocean.

2 Who did Liz call?
  a emergency services in the U.S.
  b emergency services in the UK
  c the police in the UK

B Discuss your answers in pairs. Can you explain why the incorrect options are wrong?

5 What advice do you think Liz gives to tourists after her experience?

6 ▶ 10.8 Watch or listen to the second part of the show. Which emergency service does each person talk about?

Renaldo

Ming

Lana

Fred

7 ▶ 10.8 Watch or listen again and choose the correct options to complete the sentences.

1 Renaldo, a police officer from New York, worked
   a with a patrol officer who retired last year.
   b with a police dog who helped him arrest criminals.
   c as a police dog trainer with the K-9 unit.
2 Ming, a restaurant owner in London,
   a heard a smoke alarm and called 999.
   b called 999 when she saw a fire in her restaurant.
   c watched firefighters put out a fire in her restaurant.
3 The bicyclist that Lana talks about
   a hit another man who was crossing the street.
   b was riding his bike in a dangerous way.
   c was hit by a car.
4 Fred's bike was stolen and
   a he called the police to report the theft right away.
   b the police caught the thief thanks to witnesses.
   c Kate might know who the thief is.

8 Have you heard any unusual stories about emergency services? Tell your partner.

◀H **Listening builder** **final /t/ and /d/ sounds**

English speakers don't pronounce the /t/ and /d/ sound fully at the end of a word when the next word begins with a consonant. If the next word begins with a vowel sound, the sounds are linked. *And* is often pronounced without the /d/ sound, even when the next word begins with a vowel sound.

We're talking abou(t) the emergency services.   He call(ed) the police an(d) ask(ed) them to help.

What abou(t) you? Have you heard any unusual stories about emergency services?

---

9 ▶ 10.9 Read the Listening builder. Listen and complete the sentences.

1 In the U.S., when we see a fire, want _____ crime, or _____ medical help, we call 911.
2 An emergency services dispatcher quickly _____ police in the UK.
3 I _____ as a patrol officer. _____ I was on the _____ foot.
4 He _____ and _____ many burglars, thieves, _____ criminals.
5 I _____ say something _____ emergency workers in London.

10 In pairs, discuss the questions.

1 Have you ever called or received help from an emergency service? What happened?
2 What characteristics do people need to work in the different emergency services?

Personal Best Would you like to work for an emergency service? Write five sentences explaining why/why not.

10C   Do the right thing

1   In pairs, discuss the questions.

1   Have you ever lost something on the street? Did you get it back? How?

2   Have you ever found something that someone else had lost? What did you do?

2   Read the text and choose the best option to complete the title.

a keeps it   **b** gives it back   **c** sells it online

Teenager finds movie star's wallet and _____

What would you do if you found a wallet that belonged to a famous Hollywood actor? Would you keep it, try to sell it on eBay, or return it to the owner?

This was the choice 17-year-old Tristin Budzyn-Barker had when he found a wallet in a Los Angeles restaurant. To his surprise, when he looked inside, he realized it belonged to Australian actor Chris Hemsworth, who played Thor in the *Avengers* movies. The address of Hemsworth's agent was in the wallet, so Tristin was able to return it, along with all the contents of the wallet.

When the actor got the wallet back, he had expected to find it empty, so he was amazed that the money was still in it. He invited Tristin to appear with him on a popular U.S. talk show, where Hemsworth thanked him publicly by giving him a reward – all the money in the wallet. The talk show host, Ellen DeGeneres, made Tristin's day even better by giving him another $10,000 reward.

3   ▶ 10.10   Listen to two friends talking about the story. Do they agree that Tristin did the right thing?

4   ▶ 10.10   Choose the correct options to complete the sentences. Listen again and check your answers.

1   What *would / do* you do if you *would find / found* someone's wallet?

2   *I'll / I'd* do the right thing. *I'll / I'd* definitely give it back. What about you?

3   If *I found / I'd find* a famous person's wallet, *I kept / I'd keep* it and maybe sell it online.

4   If you *keep / kept* the wallet, it *would be / was* theft!

5   If you *will give / gave* it back, the owner *will / might* give you a reward.

6   What about if you *don't / didn't* know who it belonged to? *Would / Will* you keep it then?

7   *I'd take / I took* it to the police station. It *might / would* belong to someone who really needed the money.

5   Look at the sentences in exercise 4 and answer the questions. Then read the Grammar box.

1   Are the sentences about real or hypothetical situations and their consequences?

2   Do they refer to present and future situations, or past situations?

3   Which form do we use in the *if*-clause? Which form do we use in the main clause?

Grammar second conditional, *would*, *could*, and *might*

Unlikely or impossible situations and their consequences:

If I **won** the lottery, I **wouldn't work**.   I**'d drive** to work *if* I **had** a car.
What **would** you **do** *if* someone **stole** your phone?   *If* a stranger **invited** you to a party, **would** you **go**?

Look! We can use **could** or **might** instead of *would*:
If they lived in the country, they **might** be less stressed.

Go to Grammar practice: second conditional, *would*, *could*, and *might*, page 131

6 A ▶ 10.12 Complete the sentences with the correct forms of the verbs in parentheses. Listen to Ana and Pete continue their conversation and check your answers.

1 If a salesclerk in a small store _____ you too much change, what _____ ? (give, do)
2 If he _____ me too much change, I _____ him. (give, tell)
3 _____ the salesclerk in a supermarket if he or she _____ you too much change? (tell, give)
4 If a salesclerk _____ me too much change in a supermarket, I _____ it. (give, might keep)
5 What _____ if your bank _____ $1,500 into your account by mistake? (do, put)
6 I _____ them. They _____ the mistake sooner or later. (tell, discover)

B What would you do in the situations in 6A? Discuss in pairs.

7 ▶ 10.13 **Pronunciation:** conditionals Listen to the two sentences. Notice the difference between the first conditional and the second conditional sentences.

1 If I need some help, I'll ask you.   2 If I needed some help, I'd ask you.

8 A ▶ 10.14 Listen to the sentences. Are they first or second conditional? Choose the sentence that you hear.

1 **a** I'll come if I have time.   **b** I'd come if I had time.
2 **a** If he has some money, he'll come.   **b** If he had some money, he'd come.
3 **a** If you fall, I'll catch you.   **b** If you fell, I'd catch you.
4 **a** She'll help if she has time.   **b** She'd help if she had time.

B In pairs, take turns saying one of the sentences in 8A. Your partner will identify which sentence it is.

Go to Communication practice: Student A page 164, Student B page 172

9 A Use first or second conditional forms to complete the sentences. More than one answer may be possible.

1 What's the first thing you _____ if you _____ the lottery? (might buy, win)
2 If you _____ do any job, which job _____ ? (can, choose)
3 What _____ if you _____ free time this weekend? (do, have)
4 If you _____ your favorite movie star, what _____ him/her? (meet, ask)
5 If you _____ live in any city in the world, where _____ ? (can, live)
6 If you _____ a lot of money left at the end of this month, what _____ ? (have, could do)
7 If you _____ give your 16-year-old self some advice, what _____ ? (can, say)
8 Who _____ if you _____ some help to write a job application? (ask, need)

B In pairs, ask and answer the questions in 9A.

10D For and against

1 A Look at pictures a–d. Which are the worst things to do? Number them 1–4 (1 = the worst).

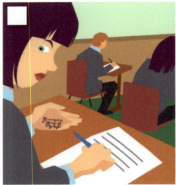

a cheating on an exam **b** traveling without a ticket **c** using a false name online **d** taking a sick day when you're not sick

B Look at the pictures again. Do you know anyone who has done any of these things? Did he/she get caught?

2 Read the first paragraph of the essay quickly. What do you think the full title of the essay is? In pairs, discuss your answers.

Everyone should _____. Discuss.

Alban Duval

A lot of people use different names on the Internet, and as a result, it is difficult to know if information online is reliable. Many social media or review websites, such as Facebook, make people use their real names so everyone can trust the information they read. However, there are some situations when people need to be anonymous.

On the one hand, if everyone used his or her real name online, the Internet might be a more reliable and pleasant place. Using a false name online allows people to be dishonest or mean. A lot of people who insult and attack other people on the Internet would never do it under their real names or in real life. Other people use a different name to write reviews of their own restaurants or stores, and criticize other businesses.

On the other hand, some people have valid reasons for not using their real names online. There are many reasons why someone would prefer to remain anonymous. Teachers, for example, often prefer not to use their real names on social media as they want to keep their personal and professional lives separate. Another example is victims of crime, who prefer to use false names so criminals are unable to contact them.

To sum up, there are valid reasons why people would choose to use false names online, and there are also dishonest reasons. I do not believe that everyone should always use his or her real name. I think people should be able to choose. In my view, the problem is not the name people use, but what they write.

---

3 In pairs, think of one argument for and one argument against the essay topic. Then read the whole essay. Were your ideas the same?

> **Skill   writing a for-and-against essay**
>
> **We write for-and-against essays to discuss both sides of an argument.**
> - Organize your essay into paragraphs. Aim for a minimum of four paragraphs: introduction, arguments for, arguments against, and the conclusion.
> - Start each paragraph with a topic sentence (a sentence that clearly introduces the topic of the paragraph).
> - Include at least one main point in each paragraph and support your topic sentence with examples.
> - Use formal language and an impersonal style. However, you can put your personal opinion in the conclusion. Use phrases like *I believe that, in my opinion, in my view*.
> - Don't use contractions, such as *isn't, don't*. Use full forms instead.

4 Read the Skill box. Then answer the questions about Alban's essay.

1 In which paragraph does Alban give his arguments for the topic?
2 In which paragraph does he give his arguments against the topic?
3 What are the main points in each for and against paragraph? What examples does he give to support them?
4 When does Alban give his personal opinion? What phrases does he use to do this?

5 Read the essay titles below. In pairs, think of arguments for and against each title, and examples to support these arguments. Use the ideas in exercise 1A and your own ideas.

1 Are exams good for learning?
2 Public transportation should be free for everyone. Discuss.
3 People should only have to work four days a week. Discuss.

> **Text builder   useful phrases for topic sentences**
>
> **On the one hand**, *smartphones can be very useful in certain situations.*
> **On the other hand**, *people tend to talk to each other less.*
> **The main advantage of** *smartphones is that they can be very useful in certain situations.*
> **However, one disadvantage** *is that people tend to talk to each other less.*
> **To sum up**, *most people take their smartphones everywhere, which has both advantages and disadvantages.*

6 Read the Text builder. Which phrases does Alban use in his topic sentences?

7 Look at the topic sentences. Which essay in exercise 5 does each sentence come from? Do the sentences introduce an argument for, an argument against, or a conclusion?

1 The main advantage is that there would be fewer cars on the road, and the air would be less polluted.
2 To sum up, not charging passengers would help people who do not have much money, but the government would have to invest a lot of money to do this.
3 On the one hand, review usually helps people understand a subject better.
4 On the other hand, limiting the number of work days per week would make it very difficult to start a new business.
5 However, one disadvantage is that they are very stressful.

8 A **PREPARE** Choose an essay title from exercise 5. Make notes of the arguments for and against.

B **PRACTICE** Use the Skill box to help you write your essay. Use topic sentences and linking phrases at the start of each paragraph.

C **PERSONAL BEST** Work in pairs. Read the topic sentences from each paragraph to your partner. Can your partner guess what the rest of the paragraph will say?

Grammar

1 Cross (**X**) out the sentence that is NOT correct.

1   a   What was your vacation in the U.S. like?
    b   What was like your vacation in the U.S.?
    c   Did you like your vacation in the U.S.?

2   a   I love going to the movies.
    b   I'd love to go to the movies tonight.
    c   I love to go to the movies tomorrow.

3   a   Eva told that she wanted to go to a museum.
    b   Eva said that she wanted to go to a museum.
    c   Eva told me that she wanted to go to a museum.

4   a   If someone stole my bag, I'd tell the police.
    b   I'd tell the police if someone stole my bag.
    c   If someone would steal my bag, I told the police.

5   a   Jonathan doesn't look like his older brother.
    b   Jonathan doesn't like his older brother.
    c   Jonathan isn't looking like his older brother.

6   a   He's worried about to miss the train.
    b   He's worried about missing the train.
    c   He wouldn't like to miss the train.

7   a   They asked me if the flight was on time.
    b   They asked me when arrived the flight.
    c   They asked me when the flight arrived.

8   a   If I had a car, I'll drive you home.
    b   I could drive you home if I had a car.
    c   If I had a car, I'd drive you home.

2 Use the words in parentheses to complete the sentences so they mean the same as the first sentence.

1   When you sing, your voice is similar to mine.
    When you sing, you _____ me. (sound)

2   I can't wait to see the next episode!
    I'm looking _____ the next episode. (forward)

3   Tom asked, "Does your girlfriend live in Boston, Adam?"
    Tom asked Adam _____ in Boston. (if)

4   We can't rent a car because I can't drive.
    If I _____ , we _____ a car. (could)

5   Can you tell me something about Adele's new album?
    What's _____ ? (like)

6   Joe couldn't go out because he didn't have enough money.
    Joe couldn't _____ out. (afford)

7   Jane said to me, "I'll meet you outside the theater."
    Jane _____ outside the theater. (said)

8   You should go to bed earlier.
    If _____ , I'd go to bed earlier. (were)

3 Complete the text with the correct form of the verbs in parentheses.

Going underground

There are two main reasons behind the current interest in underground homes. Some local governments have started **1**_____ (build) homes underground to create more space in crowded cities. **2**_____ (live) underground can also offer an escape from extreme temperatures and can provide relief from noise pollution. I decided to visit South Australia to find out what it's like to live underground.

A hundred years ago in the small mining town of Coober Pedy, miners dug cave homes in the hills **3**_____ (avoid) the intense summer heat. Today, **4**_____ (visit) the town's underground homes is a fascinating experience, and I was pleasantly surprised **5**_____ (find) there was plenty of natural light from openings in the ground above. In addition, it was like **6**_____ (be) in an air-conditioned house even though the temperature outside was 40 degrees Celsius. If I lived in Coober Pedy, or somewhere else very hot, I **7**_____ (want) to live in an underground home because it is so cool.

I met some other tourists who were staying in an underground hotel, and I asked them if they **8**_____ (enjoy) the experience. Most said that they **9**_____ (have) a wonderful night's sleep the previous night because it was so quiet. One woman told me she **10**_____ (may) even build her own underground home since her apartment **11**_____ (be) in a noisy area, and she **12**_____ (want) to live somewhere quiet.

It seems that life underground has its advantages, which more of us may experience in years to come.

Vocabulary

1 Circle the word that is different. Explain your answer.

1	boiled	fried	baked	sliced
2	steal	theft	rob	mug
3	dessert	plate	main course	appetizer
4	thief	robber	arrest	murderer
5	achievement	confusion	disappointment	government
6	rare	homemade	well-done	medium
7	lime	zucchini	garlic	asparagus
8	fork	knife	napkin	spoon

2 Match the words in the box with definitions 1–10.

> argument   leave a tip   takeout   order something   burglary
> studying   lentils   fine   protection   get the check

1 food bought from a restaurant to eat at home _____
2 these are often used in soups _____
3 entering a building illegally and stealing from it _____
4 money paid as a punishment _____
5 keeping something safe _____
6 give some money to the waiter after a meal _____
7 ask the waiter to bring you food or drink _____
8 ask for the piece of paper showing how
   much your food cost _____
9 an angry disagreement _____
10 learning in preparation for an exam _____

3 Choose the correct options to complete the sentences.

1 I usually have _____ with my cereal for breakfast.
   a olive oil   **b** yogurt   **c** soy sauce
2 I'm not going to leave a big tip because the _____
   was awful. It took hours!
   a service   **b** check   **c** atmosphere
3 I'd like to _____ a table for four for 8 p.m., please.
   a order   **b** reserve   **c** get
4 Should I put _____ carrots in the salad or sliced
   carrots?
   a grated   **b** melted   **c** rare
5 The two men _____ the house and took two
   laptops and $150 in cash.
   a mugged   **b** stole   **c** broke into
6 He has a lot of _____, so he often has ideas for
   stories.
   a imaginary   **b** imagine   **c** imagination
7 She made an important _____ when she chose to
   get a job instead of going to college.
   a information   **b** decision   **c** education
8 I'm vegan, so can I have the _____ please?
   a steak   **b** shellfish   **c** chickpeas

4 Complete the text with the words in the box.

> stolen   prison   mugging   victim   witness   arrested
> suspect   mugged   broken   burglary

Police [1]_____ a 22-year-old man outside a shopping
center yesterday afternoon. A [2]_____ said that the
man had [3]_____ a businessperson and had taken his
wallet. Fortunately, the [4]_____ of the [5]_____
wasn't badly hurt. When the police took the [6]_____
to the police station, they realized that he had previously
spent six months in [7]_____ for [8]_____ . He had
[9]_____ into a house and had [10]_____ a TV and
$400 in cash.

Personal Best

Lesson 9A
Name four adjectives that describe ways of cooking food.

Lesson 10A
Name four types of criminals.

Lesson 9A
Write four sentences about your favorite dish, using *like* in different ways.

Lesson 10A
Report three sentences or questions that people have said today.

Lesson 9B
Write a sentence using *one* and a sentence using *ones*.

Lesson 10B
Name four nouns that end with *-sion*, *-ment*, *-ation* and *-ion*.

Lesson 9C
Describe three things you did (or didn't do) the last time you went to a restaurant.

Lesson 10C
Write three second conditional sentences.

Lesson 9C
Write two sentences with *-ing* forms and two with infinitives.

Lesson 10D
Write two sentences with *On the one hand* and *On the other hand*.

Lesson 9D
Give four expressions for making and responding to suggestions.

Lesson 10D
Write a sentence starting with *To sum up*.

The natural world

11A Nature goes viral

1 Which of the natural features below does your country have? Have you visited these places?

> rainforest   mountain range   volcano   waterfall   ocean   coast   desert   jungle

Personal Best

Go to Vocabulary practice: the natural world, page 153

2 A Look at the pictures in the text. What can you see? Where do you think each picture was taken?

B Read the text and check your ideas. Which is your favorite picture? Why?

Nature goes viral
Here are four of our favorite nature photos that have gone viral.

The first photo shows the beauty of nature. Eric Nguyen took this incredible picture of a tornado in Kansas. The sun is shining through a gap in the clouds and has formed a rainbow. Tornadoes are the most violent type of storm on Earth, and there are over 1,000 tornadoes a year around the world. Many of them take place in Tornado Alley in the U.S.

This isn't a science-fiction movie – the people in the photo aren't really tiny. This is the Salar de Uyuni, the largest "salt flat" in the world, located in the southwest of Bolivia. It's completely flat – there are no hills or trees to give you a sense of perspective, so people love taking photos like this one there.

João Pereira de Souza is a bricklayer from Ilha Grande, a small island off the coast of Rio de Janeiro. One day, João found a penguin covered in oil in his backyard. He cleaned the penguin, fed him, and released him back into the Atlantic Ocean. The penguin comes back to visit João every year, and he has been named "Dindim."

This picture is a sensation on the Internet, especially among Batman fans. It's a photo of an iceberg in Newfoundland, Canada, which looks exactly like the crime-fighting superhero Batman. The photo was taken by Mike Parsons, a software engineer from Newfoundland.

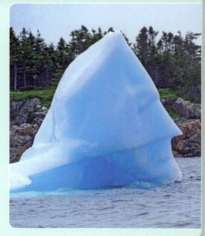

3 Complete the sentences. Check your answers in the text.

1 The _____ photo shows the beauty of nature.
2 The _____ is shining.
3 _____ are the most violent type of storm.
4 There are over 1,000 tornadoes a _____ .
5 Many take place in Tornado Alley in the _____ .
6 João Pereira de Souza is a _____ .
7 João released him back into the _____ .
8 It's the _____ salt flat in the world.
9 It's a _____ of an iceberg in Newfoundland.
10 The _____ was taken by Mike Parsons.

4 When do we use *a/an*, *the*, or no article? Match the sentences in exercise 3 with rules a–j. Then read the Grammar box.

a Use *a/an* when you mention something for the first time. _____
b Use *the* when there's only one of something. _____
c Use *the* with superlative adjectives. _____
d Use *a/an* to talk about frequency or speed. _____
e Use *the* with countries that include *united*, *republic,* and *kingdom*. _____
f Use *the* with the names of rivers, seas, and oceans. _____
g Use no article to talk about things in general. _____
h Use *the* with ordinal numbers (*first*, *second*, *third*, etc.). _____
i Use *the* to talk about something you've already mentioned. _____
j Use *a/an* to talk about somebody's job. _____

📖 **Grammar   articles**

Definite article (*the*):
*There's a car outside. **The** car's red.*
*You're **the** best person for the job.*
*Take **the** first street on the left.*
*He lives in **the** United States.*

Indefinite article (*a/an*):
*There was **a** very old man in the café.*
*I usually try to swim once **a** week.*
The speed limit is 60 km. an hour.
*He's studying to become **a** vet.*

No article:
I love documentaries about nature.
Do you like coffee?
Spiders are horrible.
I'm going to work now.

Personal Best

Go to Grammar practice: articles, page 132

5 **A** ▶11.4 **Pronunciation:** *the* Listen to the sentences. Is *the* pronounced /ðə/ or /ðiː/ before a vowel sound?

1 **The** earthquake woke us up. _____
2 Is **the** volcano still active? _____
3 **The** Atlantic Ocean is huge. _____
4 Can you see **the** sea? _____

B ▶11.4 Listen again and repeat the sentences.

6 Complete the text with *the*, *a/an*, or – (no article).

¹_____ team of designers in Seoul, ²_____ South Korea, has been working on ³_____ project to make ⁴_____ rainy days more fun. ⁵_____ project is called *Project Monsoon*, and ⁶_____ team of designers plans to use ⁷_____ special type of paint that can only be seen when ⁸_____ ground is wet. So on ⁹_____ rainy days, people would see colorful pictures of ¹⁰_____ whales, turtles, and fish instead of the usual gray streets. ¹¹_____ project was created to help ¹²_____ residents of Seoul look forward to ¹³_____ monsoon season, when most people normally stay at ¹⁴_____ home to avoid the rain.

Go to Communication practice: Student A page 164, Student B page 173

7 Work in small groups. Discuss the statements.

1 Saturday is the best night of the week to go out.
2 Women are better than men at learning languages.
3 Classical music is more relaxing than pop music.
4 You should get exercise three times a week.
5 The best things in life are free.
6 Space travel is a waste of money.
7 The Internet is the most important invention ever.

Personal Best Write a paragraph describing a photo you have seen that has "gone viral."

11B A disaster waiting to happen

1 What happens during these natural disasters? Have any of these been in the news recently?

earthquake   volcanic eruption   forest fire   flood   tsunami   hurricane

Skill   understanding the writer's purpose

When reading a text, look for clues that tell you the purpose of the whole text and parts of the text. The writer's purpose may be to:
- give advice or a warning
- give information, examples, facts, or opinions
- describe a person, event, idea, or issue
- make a comparison or contrast
- explain a reason, cause, or result

2 Read the Skill box. Then read the text quickly. What is the general purpose of the text? Choose the best option.

a to give travel advice to tourists in southern Italy
b to describe everyday life and the reasons people live near a volcano
c to warn people that volcanoes in Italy are dangerous

3 Choose the correct option to answer the questions. Why does the writer …

1 … describe an earthquake in paragraph 1?
   a to explain why a volcano erupts
   b to compare an earthquake with a volcanic eruption
   c to describe how a volcanic eruption starts

2 … describe the AD 79 eruption of Vesuvius in paragraph 1?
   a to explain why he was worried about the earthquake
   b to explain how Pompeii and Herculaneum were destroyed
   c to give examples of places that were destroyed by volcanic eruptions

3 … include the quotation "Volcanoes will do whatever they feel like" in paragraph 2?
   a to explain that it is difficult to predict when Vesuvius will erupt
   b to give an example of how the local people aren't very worried
   c to warn visitors to be prepared for a volcanic eruption at any time

4 … mention *tomatoes* and *mud baths* in paragraph 4?
   a to give information about the geography of the area
   b to give examples of good things about volcanoes
   c to compare different tourist activities

5 … talk about canceled flights in paragraph 5?
   a to explain the only negative result of the most recent eruption on Etna
   b to explain how lives were put in danger by the eruption in 2007
   c to give people advice about traveling to this volcanic area

Text builder   understanding noun phrases

The subject of a sentence is not always a single noun. Sometimes the subject is a noun phrase which has several words.
Living near Vesuvius all their lives has given them a feeling for the volcano's behavior.
In Sicily, *25% of the island's population* lives on or around Mount Etna.

4 **A** Read the Text builder. Underline the subjects of all the sentences in paragraph 6.

   B Which of the subjects that you underlined in paragraph 6 are noun phrases?

5 In pairs, think of five questions you would ask people who live near a volcano.

In the shadow of a **volcano**

by Nick Daley

1 When it starts, the floor begins to move. Cups and plates shake in kitchen cabinets. These are the signs that a volcanic eruption is coming, and it begins with an earthquake. When I felt one on my trip to Naples, in southern Italy, I felt panic, thinking that the "big one" was coming. I was terrified that the nearby volcano of Vesuvius would erupt just like it did in AD 79, destroying the towns of Pompeii and Herculaneum. Tragically, on that occasion thousands of people died.

2 This time, no eruption came. My hosts, a Neapolitan family, just smiled. Living near Vesuvius all their lives has given them a feeling for the volcano's behavior. From long experience, they know if something bad is happening. This is why nobody seems concerned. They are not alone in their relaxed attitude to the danger above their heads. "Volcanoes will do whatever they feel like," says another local resident, Ciro Russo, as he shrugs his shoulders and carries on with normal life.

3 It was my fascination with these people that drew me to Italy. Why do people choose to live under an active volcano despite knowing about the risks? Vesuvius is not even the only volcano in the country – in Sicily, 25% of the island's population lives on or around Mount Etna, another active volcano.

4 The most obvious answer to this question is that people have always lived in the area – these regions have been inhabited for thousands of years. In addition, living next to a volcano has some advantages. Chemicals in the volcanic ash create ideal conditions for agriculture, especially for tomatoes. Volcanoes also attract visitors, and that brings money. One popular tourist activity is bathing in hot mud baths on nearby volcanic islands.

5 Most important of all, the actual risk should be assessed. There hasn't been a big eruption on Mount Vesuvius since 1944. At that time, a few villages were evacuated, but older people in the area just remember roasting chestnuts on the hot magma in the streets. Etna has erupted more recently, but not enough to put lives in danger. The 2007 eruption simply caused a number of canceled flights because planes can crash if volcanic dust enters their engines (the dust is sharp, like glass).

6 People who live in the shadow of a volcano have a view of life that is different from the rest of us, and this provides an important lesson. As one elderly resident of the region says, "The volcano is part of our culture, it's part of life, and it's as beautiful as the sea." With danger so close to home, the people who live near these Italian volcanoes know how important it is to enjoy their day-to-day existence as much as possible, rather than worrying about the potential disaster that's waiting at the end of the road.

Personal Best   Write a paragraph about a natural feature that you have visited. Use some noun phrases.

11C I will survive

1 Have you ever gotten lost in the city or country? If so, what happened? Tell your partner.

2 Read the text and answer the questions.

  1 How did Ann get lost?   **2** How did she survive?   **3** How was she found?

Grandmother survives nine days lost in the wild

A 72-year-old woman and her dog have been rescued after surviving for nine days alone in the White Mountains area of Arizona.

Ann Rodgers was driving to Phoenix to visit her grandchildren when her car ran out of gas on a deserted road. She couldn't use her phone because there was no signal, so she decided to leave her car and walk to higher ground. Instead, she got lost and spent the next nine days in danger of attack by bears and mountain lions. She survived by drinking river water, eating plants, and building fires to keep warm in **freezing** temperatures.

The search started four days after Ann disappeared, when her car was found by the road. Rescue teams searched the area on foot and with helicopters, but found nothing. Two days into the search, rescuers saw Ann's dog in a canyon. A helicopter searched the area and found a large "help" sign that Ann had made out of rocks and sticks. Ann had also left a note saying that she was **starving** because she hadn't eaten, and she was going to follow the river to find a farm.

The helicopter immediately flew into the canyon and found Ann. She was **filthy** and **exhausted**, but alive. Her rescuers hadn't expected to find her alive, and believe that if she hadn't made the "help" sign, they wouldn't have found her. However, they also think that leaving her car was a mistake – if she had stayed with her car, they would have found her more quickly.

3 Look at the adjectives in **bold** in the text. Match them with definitions 1–4.

  1 very dirty   **2** very hungry   **3** very cold   **4** very tired

Go to Vocabulary practice: extreme adjectives, page 154

Personal Best

4 **A** Choose the correct option to complete the sentences about Ann's story.

  1 Ann *stayed / didn't stay* with her car.
  2 Rescuers *found / didn't find* her quickly.
  3 If Ann *had / hadn't* stayed with her car, rescuers *would / wouldn't* have found her more quickly.

B Look at sentence 3 in 4A. Answer the questions.

  1 Which clause is about a hypothetical situation in the past?
  2 Which clause is about a possible consequence of the hypothetical situation?
  3 Which clause contains a verb in the past perfect?
  4 Which clause contains *would* + *have* + past participle?

5 **A** Complete the sentence. Check your answer in the last paragraph of the text.

  If Ann _____ the "help" sign, rescuers _____ her.

B What really happened? Choose the correct options. Then read the Grammar box.

  Ann *made / didn't make* the "help" sign. The rescuers *found / didn't find* her.

📖 **Grammar**   **third conditional**

Unreal past situations and their consequences:

*If you **had asked** me, I **would have helped**.* (You didn't ask me. I didn't help)
*If I **hadn't called** you, I **wouldn't have heard** the news.* (I did call you. I heard the news.)

Look! We can put the *if* clause after the main clause. We don't use a comma:
*I wouldn't have heard the news **if I hadn't called you.***

Go to Grammar practice: third conditional, page 133

6 Match the clauses to make complete sentences.

1 If I'd studied harder,	**a** I'd have been a professional soccer player.
2 If I hadn't gone to that party,	**b** my cold would have got better.
3 If I'd saved more money,	**c** I wouldn't have forgotten to lock the door.
4 If I'd been good at sports,	**d** I would have passed the exam.
5 If I hadn't been in such a hurry,	**e** I'd have bought a car.
6 If I'd rested last weekend,	**f** I wouldn't have met my best friend.

7 **A** ▶11.7 **Pronunciation:** weak form of *have* Listen to the sentences and notice the pronunciation of *have* in *would have* and *wouldn't have*. Listen again and repeat the sentences.

1 If I'd studied harder, I would **have** passed the exam.
2 If I hadn't gone to that party, I wouldn't **have** met my best friend.
3 If I'd saved more money, I would **have** bought a car.

B Look at the sentences in 7A. Change them to make third conditional sentences that are true for you.

If I hadn't studied last weekend, I would have failed the test.

8 **A** ▶11.8   Listen to a survival expert talking about Ann's story. The expert also mentions another survival story. Why was it worse?

B ▶11.8   Complete the sentences about Ann and Victoria. Then listen again and check your answers.

1 Ann _____ if she _____ how to start a fire. (not survive, not know)
2 Victoria _____ if she _____ at night because it was so cold. (might die, sleep)
3 The rescue team _____ Victoria sooner if she _____ someone about her plans. (find, tell)
4 If Ann _____ enough gas in her car, she _____ a problem in the first place. (have, not have)
5 If they _____ a signal on their phones, both Ann and Victoria _____ for help. (have, can call)
6 If Victoria _____ some warmer clothes and food with her, she _____ so cold and hungry. (take, not be)
7 If she _____ a walking stick to her leg, she _____ her leg more. (not tie, might injure)
8 Ann _____ if she _____ near her car. (not get lost, stay)

Go to Communication practice: Student A page 164, Student B page 173

9 Think about five important things that have happened in your life. Tell your partner what would have been different in your life if these things hadn't happened. Use these ideas or your own ideas.

an exam you passed or failed   a job you applied for   a friend you met

a new hobby you started   a place you went to   an important decision you made

If I hadn't met my friend Lisa, I wouldn't have passed my English test. She's really good at English and helps me a lot.

Personal Best Write four sentences about things that happened last week and what would have happened if they had been different.

11D The great outdoors

1 Think of two of your most memorable photos of activities, trips, or vacations in the great outdoors. Describe them to your partner. Talk about:

- where the photos were taken
- what the weather was like
- who you were with
- what you were doing
- any natural features in the photos

2 ▶ 11.9 Watch or listen to the first part of *Learning Curve*. Choose the correct option to complete the sentence.

Kate wants recommendations about ...
a ... where she should go on a trip to England.
b ... where she should go for a week's vacation in the UK.
c ... which mountain range in Scotland she should visit.
d ... where she should go to escape the bad weather.

3 ▶ 11.9 Match the two parts to make complete sentences from Kate, Jack, and Simon's conversation. Watch or listen again and check.

1 I made pasta with tomatoes and herbs. Tonight's special.
2 I'd recommend
3 I love Scotland. My grandmother lives in Glasgow.
4 If I were you,
5 You should
6 Perhaps you

a You should go there.
b You really should try it.
c visit Scotland.
d could see the south coast of England.
e I wouldn't. It's too rainy!
f staying here in London and seeing places you've never seen.

🧩 Conversation builder — making recommendations

Asking for ideas
What would you recommend?
What do you think I should do?
Do you have any ideas about ... ?
Where would be the best place to ...?

Making recommendations
I'd recommend Paris / I'd recommend going to Paris.
If I were you, I'd/I wouldn't ...
Perhaps you could ...
You (really) should ...

4 Read the Conversation builder. Which recommendation phrase is the strongest?

5 In groups, ask for and make recommendations about three of the subjects.

> outdoor sports   places to relax   travel apps   saving money on transportation
> clothes to wear for traveling   staying warm/cool outdoors

6 ▶ **11.10**   Watch or listen to the second part of the show. Are the sentences true (T) or false (F)? Correct the false sentences.

   1 Simon recommends visiting the southeast of England. _____

   2 Simon is from that part of England. _____

   3 Kate makes her decision by tossing a coin. _____

   4 Simon and Jack decide that "heads" means Dover and "tails" means Scotland. _____

   5 Kate is going to drive to Glasgow. _____

> 🔧 **Skill**   **checking and clarifying information**
>
> **We often need to check or clarify information, for example, facts, someone's feelings, or what someone means.**
> - Use tag questions, e.g., *This is the train to Boston, isn't it?*
> - Say that you haven't understood, e.g., *I'm sorry, I'm not sure I understand what you mean.*
> - Summarize what the other person has said, e.g., *So what you're saying is …*

7 ▶ **11.10**   Read the Skill box. Watch or listen again. How does Kate check what Simon means when he talks about Dover?

8 **A** In pairs, order sentences a–i to make a conversation.

   a ☐ Yes, I think so. And the days are still pretty long.

   b ☐ I'm not sure I understand what you mean.

   c ☐ That's right, and sometimes you get some really hot days.

   d ☑ 1 I'm trying to plan a trip to England. When's a good time to go?

   e ☐ I mean that the evenings are still pretty light.

   f ☐ So what you're saying is that September's the best time.

   g ☐ Great! I think September sounds perfect.

   h ☐ Summer's a popular time, but it's very busy then. April and May can be pretty cold. September can be very nice, and kids are back in school by then. Winter's not a great time to go.

   i ☐ Oh, I see. And it's usually pretty mild in September, isn't it?

B ▶ **11.11**   Listen and check. Practice the conversation.

Go to Communication practice: Student A page 164, Student B page 173

9 **A** PREPARE   In pairs, choose a beautiful region or national park in your country. One student is planning a trip there and will ask for recommendations. The other student will answer with his/her opinions. Think of what you could say.

B PRACTICE   In pairs, practice your conversation. Take turns making recommendations. Check and clarify the information that you hear.

C PERSONAL BEST   Could you improve the way you make recommendations or check information? Practice again with a new partner. Talk about a different place.

Getting away

12A Dream destinations

1 Read the dictionary definitions of *go away* and *get away* and answer the questions below.

> **go away (v)**
> leave your home to spend time in a different place, usually for a vacation or a business trip

> **get away (v)**
> go somewhere on vacation because you need to escape and have a rest

1 Are you going away anywhere soon?

2 When you need to get away, where do you go?

Personal Best

Go to Vocabulary practice: phrases with *go* and *get*, page 154

2 A Complete the blog post with the correct form of phrases with *go* and *get*.

My **dream** destinations

I'm dreaming of ¹_____ away from it all, relaxing, and having some amazing experiences. Here's a list of my top five dream destinations and what I'd like to do there.

1 Costa Rica: the rainforest

I really want to ²_____ hiking in the rainforest in Costa Rica. I'd visit the Braulio Carrillo National Park and then hike alongside the crystal-clear waters of the Corinto River.

2 Canada: the Northern Lights

I'd love to travel to Canada to see the Aurora Borealis — the Northern Lights. Imagine seeing the nighttime sky full of color like that — amazing.

3 The U.S.: a classic road trip

I'd really like to ³_____ a road trip across the U.S. I'd rent a car in Chicago and drive along famous Route 66. It takes five days to ⁴_____ to California. You can't beat the freedom of the open road.

4 The Galápagos Islands: swimming with sharks

I've always wanted to ⁵_____ scuba diving around the Galápagos Islands. It would be amazing to see all the sea life there and swim with sharks!

5 Florida: Shuttle Launch Experience

I'd love to try the Shuttle Launch Experience at the Kennedy Space Center, and feel like I'm floating like an astronaut with the sensation of weightlessness.

B Would you like to go to any of these places or do these activities?

3 A ▶12.2 Listen to Paul and Lia talking about their friend Carl's blog post in exercise 2. Which two activities do Paul and Lia both want to do?

B ▶12.2 Listen again and match the statements with the replies.

1 I'm reading his blog right now.
2 I love hiking.
3 I've always wanted to see the Northern Lights.
4 I don't like the cold very much.
5 I don't really like long car rides.
6 I'd love to swim with sharks.
7 I wouldn't want to float like an astronaut.

a So have I.
b So do I.
c So am I.
d Neither do I.
e I wouldn't.
f Neither would I.
g I do.

4 **A** Look at the replies in exercise 3B. Which ones ...

1 agree with an affirmative statement?
2 agree with a negative statement?
3 disagree with an affirmative statement?
4 disagree with a negative statement?

B Choose the correct options to complete the rules. Then read the Grammar box.

1 We use *so / neither* to agree with an affirmative statement.
2 We use *so / neither* to agree with a negative statement.
3 We use an *auxiliary / main* verb in the reply.

> **Grammar** *So/Neither do I*
>
> **Agreeing:**
> "I love studying English."   "**So do I.**"
> "I haven't finished yet."   "**Neither have I.**"
> "I was at home yesterday."   "**So was I.**"
> "I'm not going away this year."   "**Neither am I.**"
>
> **Disagreeing:**
> "I didn't like the movie."   "**I did.**"
> "I'm really hungry."   "**I'm not.**"
> "I won't go there again."   "**I will.**"
> "I don't understand."   "**I do.**"

Personal Best

Go to Grammar practice: *So/Neither do I*, page 134

5 **A** ▶12.4 **Pronunciation:** auxiliary verbs and stress Listen and <u>underline</u> the stressed words. Do we stress the auxiliary verb?

1 Neither do I.
2 I will.
3 So do I.
4 Neither have I.
5 So did I.
6 I haven't.

B ▶12.4 Listen again and repeat.

Go to Communication practice: Student A page 165, Student B page 173

6 **A** Match statements 1–6 with replies a–f. Complete the replies with an auxiliary verb.

1 I've never been to the U.S.
2 I spent two weeks at the beach last year.
3 I won't go away with my family next year.
4 I wouldn't want to go on a road trip.
5 I don't like traveling by bus.
6 I really need to get away from it all.

a So _____ I. I've been so stressed out!
b I _____ ! I went to Miami last year.
c Neither _____ I. I prefer to drive.
d I _____ . I didn't get away at all.
e I _____ . We go on vacation together every year.
f Neither _____ I. I hate long car rides.

B In pairs, say the statements in 6A, changing them so they are true for you. Reply with a true answer.

A *I've never been to Europe.*   **B** *I have. I went to Spain last year.*

7 **A** Write one thing for each topic.

- an amazing place you've been to
- a place you haven't been to, but would like to visit
- something you don't like doing on vacation
- a future plan

B In pairs, discuss what you wrote in 7A. Agree or disagree and ask more questions.

A *I don't like playing sports when I'm on vacation.*   **B** *Neither do I – vacations are for relaxing! What do you like doing?*

Personal Best Write replies to the statements in exercise 3B. The replies should be true for you.

Learning Curve

12B Fly away

1 A Look at the e-ticket below and answer the questions.

1 What time does the flight **take off** from Los Angeles and **land** in New York?
2 What time do passengers have to **board** the plane? At which **gate**?
3 What's the passenger's seat number? Is it an **aisle seat** or a **window seat**?

LOS ANGELES → NEW YORK
APRIL 16, 2017

LAX 12:00 PM   **JFK** 4:15 PM

FLIGHT **BC463** GATE **8A** SEAT **17A** window BOARDING **11:45 AM**

E-TICKET

B What do the words in **bold** in exercise 1A mean?

Personal Best

Go to Vocabulary practice: air travel, page 155

2 Discuss the questions in pairs.

1 Do you like flying? Why/Why not?   2 What are the best and worst things about traveling by plane?

3 A ▶ **12.6** Watch or listen to the first part of *Learning Curve* and complete the summary.

Today's show is about how people feel about flying. Penny and Ethan both get a little ¹_____ before a flight.

Ethan mentions that ²_____ % of people are afraid of flying. Symptoms of this fear are feeling ³_____ and panicking. To help these people, there are courses at ⁴_____ where people can "practice" flying.

Some people, however, simply don't want to travel by plane. They prefer to travel shorter distances by other means of transportation and stay longer in a place to explore the area. This is called "⁵_____ travel."

B ▶ **12.6** Compare your answers in pairs. Watch or listen again and check your answers.

4 ▶ **12.7** How do we know that Ethan has the same opinion as Penny about flying? Listen and complete the conversation. Then read the Skill box.

Penny I love flying. It's exciting. But I also get a little nervous when I'm about to fly.

Ethan _____ , Penny. And that's very common. Most people feel a bit nervous before they fly.

 Skill identifying agreement between speakers

There are a number of ways English speakers show agreement with each other. Recognizing these will help you follow a conversation.
- Listen for what the first person's opinion is, and then listen carefully to how the second person responds.
- Listen for ways of agreeing: *So do I. Neither do I. Me too. I do, too. Me neither. It sure is. It certainly is. True. Exactly. Absolutely.*
- Sometimes the first person invites agreement: *You like flying, don't you? (No, I don't.)*

Hanna

Monroe

Anoush

5 ▶12.8 Watch or listen to the second part of the show. Penny talks to Hanna, Monroe, and Anoush. Which person ...

1 has arrived at his/her destination airport? _____
2 is going somewhere warmer? _____
3 wants to change his/her seat assignment? _____
4 had to change his/her travel plans due to bad weather? _____
5 works for an airline? _____
6 is going to work during the flight? _____

6 ▶12.8 Watch or listen again. How do the speakers agree with Penny? Complete the responses.

> That's a long flight!

> Monroe: ¹Yeah, _____ _____ _____

> That sounds a bit stressful!

> Anoush: ² _____

> They are very patient, aren't they?

> Anoush: ³Yes, _____ _____ _____

7 In pairs, say these phrases slowly, separating each word. Then say them quickly, linking each word. What happens between the words marked with a link?

1 So do I.   2 I do as well.   3 I agree.   4 No, he isn't.

⊹ Listening builder   linking: /w/ and /y/

When a word ends in a vowel sound and the next word starts with a vowel sound, we usually link the words together by adding an extra sound.
When a word ends in /u:/, /ow/, or /aw/, we link it using /w/:

/w/   /w/   /w/
Who are you?   Go away.   How are you?

When a word ends in /ey/, /iy/,or /ay/, we link it using /y/:

/y/   /y/   /y/
Say it.   She agrees.   I understand.

---

8 **A** ▶12.9 Read the Listening builder. Listen to the phrases in exercise 7. Which sounds are used between the words marked with a link, /w/ or /y/?

B ▶12.9 Listen again and repeat the phrases.

9 In pairs, discuss which of these things you prefer.

1 aisle seats or window seats
2 taking off or landing
3 setting off or arriving back home
4 traveling by plane or "slow travel"
5 traveling during the day or at night
6 being the passenger or being the driver/pilot

12C Around the world

1 In pairs, answer the questions.

   1 Do you ever watch TV game shows? Which ones?

   2 Do you try to answer the questions? If so, do you often get them right?

2 Read the instructions for the game show. Would you be a good contestant on the show? Why/Why not?

9.00 p.m. Channel 7

What on Earth?

In this popular game show, the teams see a photo of a famous place, building, or object from around the world. They get three clues, and guess where or what the photo is. They can ask for more clues if they can't guess, but the fewer clues they ask for, the more points they get!

3 A Look at the three pictures. Can you guess what each one shows and where they are?

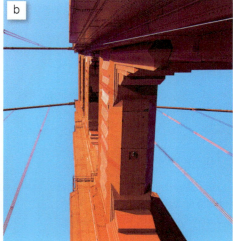

B ▶ **12.10** Listen to three pairs of contestants on the game show. Were any of your answers correct?

4 A Look at the sentences the contestants said. Which pictures were they talking about?

   1 It must be the Golden Gate Bridge.

   2 It must be some kind of statue.

   3 It can't be the White House.

   4 It can't be London.

   5 It might be somewhere in Eastern Europe.

   6 It might be the White House.

B Match the deductions in 4A with the information the contestants used to make the deductions.

   a It's pretty.

   b The clue was "it's not a capital city."

   c It's not white!

   d It's a bridge with a color in its name.

   e It looks a bit like a head.

   f It has a color in its name.

5 Look at the deductions in exercise 4A again. What do *must*, *might*, and *can't* mean? Match deductions 1–6 with meanings a–c. Then read the Grammar box.

   a I think this is possibly true. _____ _____

   b I'm sure this is true. _____ _____

   c I'm sure this isn't true. _____ _____

📖 **Grammar**   **modals of deduction**

Something you think is true:
*You've been traveling since five o'clock this morning. You **must** be tired.*
Something you don't think is true:
*He **can't** be a doctor. He's much too young.*
Something you think is possibly true:
*Carla isn't here. She **might** be studying in the library since she has an exam tomorrow.*

Look! We also use *may* or *could* for something that is possibly true:
*James isn't here. He **may** be at home, or he **could** be at the gym.*

Go to Grammar practice: modals of deduction, page 135

6   Match sentences 1–6 with replies a–f.

1   I think Marta just arrived.
2   How old is Jack?
3   Do you think the neighbors are at home?
4   Ricardo is in such good shape!
5   Why didn't Helen eat any steak?
6   Tina's not answering her phone.

a   I don't know. She **might be** a vegetarian.
b   I know. He **must get** a lot of exercise.
c   He's in college, so he **must be** at least eighteen.
d   It **can't be** her. She said she wasn't coming.
e   She **might be** swimming.
f   They **can't be**. All the lights are off.

7   **A** ▶ 12.12 **Pronunciation:** sentence stress Listen to sentences a–f in exercise 6. Look at the words in **bold**. Which do we stress most, the modal verb or the main verb?

B   In pairs, practice saying the sentences and answers in exercise 6.

8   Complete the conversation in a restaurant with *might*, *must*, and *can't*.

A   Oh look, there's the waiter, carrying a tray. There's nobody else in here, so that ¹_____ be our food.
B   Didn't you order a pizza, though? That looks like pasta. It ²_____ be for us.
A   Why is it taking so long? We're the only people here – the kitchen ³_____ be that busy!
B   It hasn't been that long. There ⁴_____ be a problem, or the chef ⁵_____ be taking a coffee break. You didn't have any breakfast, did you? You ⁶_____ be starving!

Go to Communication practice: Student A page 165, Student B page 174

9   Look at the two pictures. In pairs, use modals of deduction to talk about the pictures. Who are the people? Where are they? What is happening?

a

b

Personal Best   Work with a partner. Show each other photos on your cell phones and make deductions about the photos.

12D Five-star review

1 Discuss the questions in pairs.

    1 Have you ever had a very good or bad experience of a hotel, restaurant, or organized activity? What happened?

    2 Have you ever read or written online reviews? What for?

2 Read three online reviews quickly. How many stars (out of five) do you think each reviewer gave?

The Sands Hotel, San Francisco

We stayed at The Sands Hotel to celebrate spring break in our final year of college. We were looking for a budget hotel downtown, and we couldn't be happier with our experience.

It's a two-star hotel, so we had expected the building to be pretty old with very small rooms, but, actually, all the rooms were bright and modern. It was pretty hot, though, and, unfortunately, they don't have air conditioning.

As this is a budget hotel, these are obviously not luxury accommodations, but it would be perfect for people who are looking for an affordable place to stay in a central location.

La Gamba Tapas, Minnesota

My classmates and I went to La Gamba Tapas for our end-of-year meal last month. We were really looking forward to it, but I'm sorry to say that it wasn't a good experience.

They had told us that we wouldn't need a reservation, but, in fact, we had to wait forty minutes to get a table. The food wasn't bad, but we were told by our very rude waiter that they had run out of a lot of dishes. We had wanted to try their famous garlic shrimp – hopefully, next time they will have some. If we ever go back, that is!

All in all, the food at La Gamba Tapas is good, but I wouldn't recommend it to people who value good service.

Horse & Holiday, Alberta, Canada

This summer, my boyfriend and I decided to go on a three-day horseback riding trip in the Rocky Mountains. The trip was great – it was well organized with helpful guides, and the views of the mountains were breathtaking.

According to the website, the trip is for riders of all abilities, but I had never ridden before, and I found it really difficult. Luckily, they were very sympathetic when I decided halfway through that I wanted to stop, and they arranged for a van to take me to the hostel.

People who ride well and really enjoy the great outdoors would have the trip of a lifetime, but it's definitely not for beginners.

🔧 **Skill**   **writing an online review**

We write a review to give our personal opinions about a product or service.
- Describe your expectations before. Use phrases like *we had expected ...*, *according to the website ...* .
- Describe what really happened. Use phrases like *in fact ...*, *(but) actually ...* .
- Make a recommendation about who the product or service would be good for. Use phrases like *perfect for ...*, *not really suitable for ...* .

3 Read the Skill box. Answer questions 1–3 for each of the three reviews.
   1 What were the reviewer's expectations?
   2 What actually happened?
   3 According to each reviewer, who would or wouldn't enjoy the experience?

4 Find examples of positive and negative opinions in the three reviews.

positive	negative

🧩 **Text builder**   **adverbs of attitude**

We use adverbs of attitude to say what we think about something.
*We had dinner at a famous steak restaurant. **Surprisingly**, they had vegetarian dishes.*
*I had heard great things about the hotel, but, **unfortunately**, it had closed the previous month.*
*The waiter was very rude. **Clearly**, he had more important things to do than serve us!*

Look! Adverbs of attitude usually go at the beginning of a clause or sentence.

5 Read the Text builder. Complete the sentences with adverbs. Then check your answers in the reviews.
   1 It was pretty hot, though, and, _____ , they don't have air conditioning.
   2 As this is a budget hotel, these are _____ not luxury accommodations.
   3 We had wanted to try their famous garlic shrimp – _____ , next time they will have some.
   4 _____ , they were very sympathetic when I decided halfway through that I wanted to stop.

6 Match sentences 1–6 with a–f.
   1 According to the guidebook, White Shores was the best beach in the area.
   2 The restaurant looked old and dirty outside.
   3 The restaurant was the most famous one in town.
   4 I left my passport in the hotel.
   5 We had wanted to visit the castle in the Old Town.
   6 The bicycle tour lasts six hours.

   a Unfortunately, it closed at 4 p.m., and we got there at 5.
   b Obviously, it was also the most expensive.
   c Sadly, it was crowded, and the sea was polluted.
   d Clearly, you have to be in very good shape to go on it.
   e Luckily, the receptionist found it and gave it back.
   f Surprisingly, we had the best meal of our lives there.

7 A **PREPARE** Think about a hotel, restaurant, or service that you had a good or bad experience with. Make notes about why it was good or bad.

B **PRACTICE** Use the Skill box to help you write an online review.

C **PERSONAL BEST** Exchange reviews with your partner. Would you visit the place in your partner's review? Why/Why not?

Grammar

1 Choose the correct options to complete the sentences.

1. **A** What does he do for a living? **B** He's _____ airline pilot.
   a the   b –   c an

2. If I _____ up late, I would have arrived in time for the meeting.
   a wouldn't have woken   b hadn't woken
   c didn't wake

3. **A** I can't play tennis very well. **B** Neither _____ .
   a can I.   b do I.   c can't I.

4. Only 10% of people pass their driving test the first time, so it _____ be difficult.
   a can   b must   c can't

5. _____ earthquakes are pretty common in Japan.
   a The   b An   c –

6. If she'd taken her umbrella to work, she _____ so wet.
   a wouldn't have gotten   b wouldn't get
   c hadn't gotten

7. **A** I wouldn't want to live in a large city. **B** Oh, I _____ .
   a like   b would   c wouldn't

8. Lucy _____ be a vegetarian. She had steak for dinner last night.
   a can't   b must   c can

2 Use the structures in parentheses to complete the sentences so they mean the same as the first sentence.

1. He's an actor. I saw him on that talk show. (definite article)
   He's _____ I saw on that talk show.

2. I didn't know it was a secret so I told her. (third conditional)
   If I _____ it was a secret, I _____ her.

3. **A** I really enjoyed the movie.   **B** I enjoyed it, too. (so)
   A I really enjoyed the movie.   **B** _____

4. I'm sure this isn't Steve's car because his car's red. (modal of deduction)
   This _____ Steve's car because his car's red.

5. We go on vacation in April and September. (indefinite article)
   We go on vacation _____ year.

6. She worked 50 hours last week, so she was exhausted on the weekend. (third conditional)
   She _____ exhausted on the weekend if she _____ 50 hours last week.

7. **A** He hasn't seen the game yet.   **B** I haven't seen it, either. (neither)
   A He hasn't seen the game yet.   **B** _____ .

8. It's possible that David is at work. (modal of deduction)
   David _____ be at work.

3 Choose the correct options to complete the text.

Is that e-mail genuine?

We've all heard stories about [1] *the / –* people who trick others into giving them money or personal information. I wanted to learn how to protect myself online, so I asked for advice from Bill Young, [2] *a / the* journalist for a consumer magazine.

Bill, how can we protect ourselves from [3] *the / –* scammers?

Well, [4] *the / –* first thing to do is to be aware that they exist. Don't reply to e-mails from people you don't know – they may not be genuine. I did once, and I began receiving twenty scam e-mails every day. If I hadn't replied, I wouldn't [5] *had / have* ended up on the scammer's list of confirmed e-mail addresses. I didn't give the scammers my bank information, though, which is what they were asking for.

Yes, my elderly neighbor recently got [6] *an / the* e-mail that looked like it was from her bank, asking for information about her account. She thought, "It [7] *must / can't* be from the bank," so she sent the information, and a lot of money was stolen from her account. If she'd known more about scammers, she [8] *must / might* not have believed that the e-mail was genuine. Now she wants to know all about them, and [9] *so / neither* do I!

Good! If you get an unexpected e-mail, remember that it [10] *can't / could* be fake. And, just as important, remember to change your passwords regularly, and always use different passwords for different accounts.

Vocabulary

1 Circle the word that is different. Explain your answer.

1	exhausted	miserable
	starving	gorgeous
2	rainbow	jungle
	forest	desert
3	departure board	gate
	take off	departure lounge
4	show your passport	check in
	pack	go through security
5	iceberg	hail
	tornado	hurricane
6	fantastic	filthy
	gorgeous	hilarious
7	earthquake	storm
	monsoon	flood
8	go to bed	go to school
	go home	go traveling

2 Match the words in the box with definitions 1–8.

> carry-on bag   hail   get somewhere   flight attendant
> enormous   boarding pass   tiny   coast

1 arrive at a place   _____
2 a person that looks after the passengers on
  a plane   _____
3 very small   _____
4 a bag you can bring with you on a plane   _____
5 you show this when you get on a plane   _____
6 the area of land next to the sea   _____
7 small balls of ice that fall from the sky   _____
8 extremely large   _____

3 Complete the sentences with the words in the box.

> hurricane   canyon   away   furious
> starving   hilarious   glacier   hill

1 We had a great view from the top of the _____ .
2 That romantic comedy is absolutely _____ .
3 I haven't been _____ this year. I need a vacation!
4 She was _____ when she saw that her neighbor had
  damaged her new car.
5 The _____ is 15 km. long, about 300 m. deep, and
  there's a river at the bottom.
6 I didn't have any lunch today, so I'm absolutely
  _____ . Let's have dinner now.
7 We were able to go inside the _____ and see the
  beautiful shapes of the ice.
8 The storms and strong winds during the _____ killed
  two people.

4 Choose the correct options to complete the text.

Marrakech, the Sahara, and the Atlas Mountains

I went **1**_for / on_ vacation to Morocco last year with some friends.
We spent the first day in Marrakech, where we went **2**_on / to_
a guided tour around the old town. On the second day, we
decided to go **3**_for / on_ a trip to the **4**_jungle / desert_, where
we rode camels across the sand. It was fall, so although it was
pretty hot during the day, it wasn't **5**_boiling / freezing_ like
in the summer. The day after our visit to the Sahara, we
6_went on hiking / went hiking_ in the Atlas Mountains. The view
from the top of Mount Toubkal was **7**_fantastic / hilarious_, but we
8_went / got_ really cold, so we didn't stay there long. We didn't
get back to Marrakech until after midnight, and I felt absolutely
9_gorgeous / exhausted_, so I went **10**_to / in_ bed and slept for
twelve hours.

Personal Best

Lesson 11A
Name three types of extreme weather.

Lesson 12A
Name two phrases with _go for_ and two with _go on_.

Lesson 11A
Write three sentences about the natural world: one with _a/an_, one with _the_, and one with a noun with no article.

Lesson 12A
Write three sentences that could come before "So would I," "Neither did I," and "I haven't."

Lesson 11B
Write two sentences beginning with a noun phrase.

Lesson 12B
Name three things you can find in an airport.

Lesson 11C
Name five extreme adjectives.

Lesson 12C
Write three sentences about experiences you haven't had. Use modals of deduction, e.g., _Skiing must be fun._

Lesson 11C
Write three third conditional sentences.

Lesson 12C
Write three sentences about what people are doing now. Use modals of deduction, e.g., _My sister might be having dinner._

Lesson 11D
Give two expressions for making recommendations.

Lesson 12D
Write three sentences using _fortunately_, _unluckily_, and _hopefully_.

7A The passive

 7.4

Thousands of movies **are made** every year.
The main character **was played** by Emily Blunt.
The book **has been made** into a movie.
He **was being interviewed** for the role when I called him.
Her new movie **will be released** later this year.

In active sentences, the focus is on the person or thing that does the action.

My friend Robert is repairing my bike.
Maria Jones wrote that book.

In passive sentences, the focus is on the action itself or on the thing that the action affects.

My bike is being repaired by my friend Robert.
That book was written by Maria Jones.

We often use the passive if we don't know who did the action, or if it isn't important who did the action.

The window was broken last night.
Over a million cars are made here every year.

We can use *by* in a passive sentence to say who does an action. We often use *by* when the person who does the action is new information.

The Harry Potter books are popular all over the world. They were written by J. K. Rowling.

We form the passive with a form of the verb *be* + past participle. We can use the passive with all tenses, forms, and modal verbs.

	active	passive
simple present	I usually clean it every day.	It is usually cleaned every day.
simple past	They arrested him this morning.	He was arrested this morning.
present perfect	They've completed the project.	The project has been completed.
present continuous	He is feeding the cat.	The cat is being fed.
will	We will finish the report.	The report will be finished.
past continuous	They were repairing the road.	The road was being repaired.
modal verbs	You should answer all the questions.	All the questions should be answered.

We make negatives and questions in the usual way with the negative form or the question form of the verb *be*.

He wasn't arrested.
Was he arrested?
It hasn't been completed.
Has it been completed?

1 Choose the correct options to complete the sentences.

1 She will *be met / meet* at the airport by the Prime Minister.
2 Picasso *was painted / painted* "Guernica" in 1937.
3 A new library is *being built / building* at the university.
4 The movie *directed / was directed* by Christopher Nolan.
5 The band has *sold / been sold* over 2 million copies of their new album.
6 Tickets for their next concert can *buy / be bought* online.
7 They were *being built / building* a new airport when I lived in Warsaw.
8 All the doors should *lock / be locked* when you leave the building.
9 These days, most of the world's computers *are made / make* in China.
10 I'm not sure where the next Olympic Games will *hold / be held*.

2 Rewrite the sentences in the passive.

1 He wrote the book in 2007.
_____ in 2007.
2 They have sold all the tickets for the concert.
All the tickets for the concert _____ .
3 Can you watch that movie on Netflix?
_____ that movie _____ on Netflix?
4 They're making a lot of science-fiction movies these days.
A lot of science-fiction movies _____ these days.
5 They aren't going to release their new game until next year.
Their new game _____ until next year.
6 They make cars at that factory.
Cars _____ at that factory.
7 When we arrived at the hotel, they were cleaning our room.
When we arrived at the hotel, our room
_____ .
8 They will send the information to you soon.
The information _____ to you soon.
9 They repaired my TV last week.
My TV _____ last week.
10 The fire completely destroyed the hotel.
The hotel _____ by _____ .

◀ Go back to page 59

7C Modals of ability and possibility

 7.10

I **could ride** a bike when I was four years old.
We **couldn't watch** our favorite show because the TV broke.
I'**ll be able to go** on tour with my band when I finish college.
I **wasn't able to go** to the concert because I was sick.
My dad **hasn't been able to play** squash since he hurt his knee.

can and could

We use *can/can't* and *could/couldn't*:

- to say that somebody has or had the ability to do something.
  He can play the piano really well.
  I couldn't drive five years ago.

- to say that it is or was possible to do something.
  I have my car here, so I can drive you to the station.
  I can't talk to you right now – I'll call you tonight.
  I couldn't use my cell phone when I was in the country – there was no signal.

- with verbs of the senses, such as *hear* and *see*.
  I can't hear you very well. Please speak more loudly.
  It was very foggy, and I couldn't see the cars in front of me.

be able to

We also use *be able to* + base form to talk about ability and possibility. It sounds a little more formal than *can* or *could*. We can use *be able to* with all tenses, forms, and with modal verbs.

Are you able to speak any foreign languages?
I wasn't able to finish the report yesterday.
She's never been able to swim very well.
Sorry, but I won't be able to come to the party tonight.
We love being able to sleep late on weekends.
I'd like to be able to speak Italian.

> **Look!** We can't use *can* with most tenses, structures, or modal verbs. We use *be able to*, instead.
> *I will be able to go to college if I pass my exams.* NOT ~~I will can go to college ...~~
> *I'd like to be able to play the guitar.* NOT ~~I'd like to can play the guitar.~~

We can use both *would you be able to* or *could you* to make polite requests.

Could you open the window, please?
Would you be able to pick up some milk later?

1 Choose the correct options to complete the sentences.

  1 I *can't / couldn't* speak to my father yesterday.
  2 I*'ve been able to / could* paint since I was a child.
  3 I'm sorry, but I won't *can / be able to* meet you for lunch tomorrow.
  4 Have you *could / been able to* speak to John yet?
  5 I love *can / being able to* stay in bed all morning.
  6 Maria says she'll *can / be able to* come for dinner.
  7 I'd like to *be able to / can* speak Chinese.
  8 You should *can / be able to* find a cab outside.

2 Complete the sentences with affirmative (+) and negative (–) forms of *be able to*.

  1 I'd love _____ walk to work, but it's too far away. (+)
  2 I _____ make any calls on my phone since yesterday. (–)
  3 I'm afraid that I _____ come to the meeting tomorrow. (–)
  4 The doctor _____ see you yesterday, but he's free today. (–)
  5 If I finish all my work today, I _____ go out tonight. (+)
  6 I've always _____ make new friends easily. (+)

3 Complete the text with the correct form of *can*, *could*, or *be able to* and the verbs in parentheses. There may be more than one answer.

My dad's Irish, my mom's Mexican, and I grew up in Belgium, so I've always **1**_____ (speak) different languages, plus I studied Russian and Swedish in college. At first, learning Russian was difficult as I **2**_____ (not understand) the alphabet, but I speak it well now. I travel a lot for my job, and I really love **3**_____ (talk) to local people in restaurants and markets – in my opinion, you **4**_____ (not get) to know a country if you don't make an effort to understand its language. I'd like to learn Mandarin as I'm going to Beijing for work next year. There's a Mandarin course at my local language school in May, so I'll **5**_____ (take) classes, and this time next year, I might **6**_____ (have) a conversation when I go to the market in Beijing!

◀ Go back to page 63

8A Tag questions

 8.7

You don't live in Chicago, **do you**?
Emma went to Harvard, **didn't she**?
Your parents weren't at the party last weekend, **were they**?
I'll see you tomorrow at the concert, **won't I**?
You've never been to Canada, **have you**?
They should be here by now, **shouldn't they**?

We often use a statement with a tag question when we think we know something but we want to check.

You're from Mexico, aren't you? = I think you're from Mexico. Is that right?
He doesn't speak Arabic, does he? = I don't think he speaks Arabic. Is that right?

We also use tag questions to start a conversation or to encourage somebody to speak.

It's a hot day, isn't it?
You've just bought a new car, haven't you?

With affirmative statements, we use a negative tag question. With negative statements, we use an affirmative tag question.

+	−
His name was Juan,	wasn't it?
It will be sunny later,	won't it?

−	+
We aren't late,	are we?
They didn't come,	did they?

To form a tag question, we use an auxiliary or modal verb followed by a pronoun. If the statement already contains an auxiliary or modal verb, we use it in the tag question.

We're meeting at 8:30, aren't we?
It won't rain this afternoon, will it?
The children should go to bed early tonight, shouldn't they?
Sara can't play volleyball with us on the weekend, can she?
Tim hasn't lived here very long, has he?

In the present or simple past, we make the tag question using *do, does,* or *did*.

They like Italian food, don't they?
The waiter speaks Spanish, doesn't he?
Sami spent three months in Beijing, didn't he?
You didn't like that concert, did you?

Look! We only use pronouns in tag questions. All names and nouns change to *he, she, it,* or *they*.
John plays tennis, doesn't he? NOT ~~John plays tennis, doesn't John?~~
Paris is very expensive, isn't it? NOT ~~Paris is very expensive, isn't Paris?~~

1 Match statements 1–10 with tag questions a–j.

1 Mark's coming tonight, _____
2 Michael's been to Paris before, _____
3 We shouldn't come early, _____
4 You'll help me tonight, _____
5 Tom and Dan can't speak Chinese, _____
6 You like soccer, _____
7 Sarah called you this morning, _____
8 Karl isn't here, _____
9 She didn't pass her exams, _____
10 The exam won't be easy, _____

a didn't she?
b don't you?
c is he?
d isn't he?
e should we?
f will it?
g did she?
h hasn't he?
i won't you?
j can they?

2 Complete the sentences with tag questions.

1 Surfing's an exciting sport, _____ ?
2 They're going to lose, _____ ?
3 Tina hasn't left yet, _____ ?
4 You don't know the rules, _____ ?
5 You went running on the weekend, _____ ?
6 Steven is working tonight, _____ ?
7 It wasn't a great game, _____ ?
8 We can go out for dinner tonight, _____ ?
9 The Jamaicans won't win this race, _____ ?
10 We have to show our passports, _____ ?
11 You've been waiting for ages, _____ ?
12 You used to go to that school, _____ ?

◀ Go back to page 67

8C Modals of obligation and advice

 8.13

You **have to take off** your shoes before you go into the temple.
Visitors **must park** only in the visitor parking lot.
We **don't have to work** today. It's Saturday.
You **can't give** chocolate to the dog. It's very bad for him.
I **had to go** to the doctor because I was having stomach pains.
You **should have** a more balanced diet.

have to and *must*

We generally use *have to* to talk about obligation and rules. In written rules, and in very strong statements, we can also use *must*.

I have to drive to the station because my wife's waiting for me.
You have to buy a ticket before you leave the parking lot.
You have to/must take your passport with you when you travel abroad.

We normally don't use *must* in conversation unless the obligation is very strong.

You must see a doctor immediately!

There is no past or future form of *must*, and we don't usually use *must* in questions. In these cases, we use a form of *have to* instead.

Yesterday I had to work until 8 p.m.
He'll have to find a job when he finishes college next year.
Do we have to do all the exercises or just the first one?

don't have to or *can't?*

Don't have to and *can't* have very different meanings. We use *don't have to* to say that something isn't necessary.

You don't have to pay to go by bus. Public transportation is free on Sundays.

We use *can't* to say something is prohibited.

You can't speak during the exam.

> **Look!** In spoken English, we can use *can't* or *not allowed to* to say that something isn't permitted because of a rule or a law. In written English, we use *not allowed to*.
> *You can't take photos inside the art gallery* (spoken).
> *Visitors aren't allowed to take photos inside the art gallery* (spoken or written).

should/shouldn't

We use *should* to give advice and recommendations or to say if we think that something is a good idea or a bad idea.

You should go to the gym two or three times a week.
You shouldn't eat so much fast food.

1 Choose the correct options to complete the sentences.

1 It's after midnight. I think you *can / should* go home by taxi.
2 I'm sorry I'm late. I *should / had to* take my sister to the airport.
3 I haven't seen Helen for ages. I *can / have to* call her soon to catch up.
4 You *can't / don't have to* come to the supermarket with me. I can go by myself.
5 I *don't have to / can't* go to work early today because my first meeting starts at 11 a.m.
6 You *shouldn't / have to* eat so fast – it's bad for your digestion.
7 You *don't have to / can't* park your car in front of that garage.
8 We *don't have to / can't* drive downtown. There's a very convenient bus.
9 My children *have to / can* wear a school uniform.
10 All arriving passengers *must / can* have their passports ready.

2 Complete the second sentences with the correct form of *have to*, *can*, or *should* so they have the same meaning as the first sentences. There may be more than one answer.

1 It's not necessary to hurry – there's plenty of time.
We _____ to hurry – there's plenty of time.
2 You aren't allowed to use your phone in the library.
You _____ use your phone in the library.
3 It's not a good idea to drink coffee before you go to bed.
You _____ drink coffee before you go to bed.
4 It will be necessary to stay at the airport hotel because we have an early flight.
We _____ stay at the airport hotel because we have an early flight.
5 I think it's really important for me to visit Grandma tomorrow because it's her birthday.
I really _____ visit Grandma tomorrow because it's her birthday.
6 I think it's a good idea for us to buy a bigger car.
We _____ buy a bigger car.
7 You aren't allowed to ride a motorcycle without a helmet.
You _____ ride a motorcycle without a helmet.
8 Last week, it was necessary for me to go to the hospital for a check-up.
Last week, I _____ go to the hospital for a check-up.
9 I think it's really important for us to invite Bill and Donna for dinner soon.
We really _____ invite Bill and Donna for dinner soon.
10 It's not necessary to pay to enter that museum – it's free.
You _____ pay to enter that museum – it's free.

◀ Go back to page 71

127

9A Uses of *like*

▶ 9.5

I **don't like eating** takeout.
Would you **like** a cup of tea?
Saul is **just like** his dad.

That **sounds like** a good idea.
What**'s** Japanese food **like**?
What **does** your new girlfriend **look like**?

like + verb or noun

We use the verb *like* + *-ing* or + noun to talk about preferences. We can also use *like* + infinitive.

I like listening/to listen to music.
Did he like the concert?
I think he'll like the food in that restaurant.
I didn't like that dessert.

would like

We use *would like* + infinitive or + noun to make polite offers and requests. We also use *would like* to talk about something we want to have or do. It is more polite than using the verb *want*. We usually contract it to *I'd/we'd like*.

Would you like a glass of water?
Would you like to sit down?
I'd like a chicken salad, please.
I'd like to go to Paris one day.
We'd like to try that Italian restaurant.

like (preposition)

We also use *like* as a preposition. It means "similar to." *Just like* means "exactly the same as."

Sarah is like her mother. = Sarah and her mother have a similar personality.
His car is just like mine. = His car is exactly the same as mine.

We often use the preposition *like* with verbs of the senses (*look, sound, taste, feel, smell,* etc.) and the verb *seem*. For verbs of the senses, we can use *just like* if something is exactly the same.

Your perfume smells like lemon.
That seems like a good idea.
This tastes just like chicken!

We use the phrase *feel like* + *-ing* to mean "want to do," especially when we're making plans.

What do you feel like doing tonight? = What do you want to do tonight?
I don't feel like going to the movies. = I don't want to go to the movies.

What ... like?

We use *what* + *be like* to ask for a description of something or someone.

What was the movie like?
What's that new restaurant like?

Look! We use *What's he/she like?* to ask about someone's character or personality, not his or her appearance. We use *What does he/she look like?* to ask about someone's appearance.
What's Tanya like?
She's very nice, but she's rather shy.

What does she look like?
She's very pretty, and she has short brown hair.

---

1 Put the words in the correct order to make sentences and questions.

1 party / what / Sarah's / like / was / ?
_____

2 in / like / park / my / having / I / the / lunch
_____

3 feel / going / you / like / do / tonight / out / ?
_____

4 this / like / to / movies / weekend / to / I'd / the / go
_____

5 brother / like / Martina's / does / what / look / ?
_____

6 coffee / you / a / like / of / would / cup / ?
_____

7 teacher / is / new / like / what / your / English / ?
_____

8 bigger / move / a / Maria / like / to / would / to / apartment
_____

9 Beyoncé / like / just / she / sounds
_____

10 please / reserve / like / double / a / room / I'd / to
_____

2 Complete the conversation with the words in the box.

sounds   feel (x2)   I'd   do   would   like (x2)

A Hi, Julia. Are you hungry? **1**_____ you like to go somewhere for lunch?
B Sure. Where do you **2**_____ like going?
A **3**_____ you like Greek food?
B No, I don't, not really. I think I'd **4**_____ to go to an Italian place. I **5**_____ like having pizza today.
A That **6**_____ like a good idea. What about Luigi's, then?
B I've never been to Luigi's. What are their pizzas **7**_____ ?
A They're delicious! But I had one last week, so today I think **8**_____ like to have a pasta dish.
B Great. Let's go!

◀ Go back to page 77

9C -ing forms and infinitives

 9.11

Eating out every week can be expensive.
I always go running **after coming** home from work.
That woman **keeps looking** at me. Do you know her?
It's really important **to leave** a tip in the U.S.
I decided **to become** a vegetarian three years ago.
I called the restaurant **to reserve** a table for lunch.

We use the -ing form:

• as the subject of a sentence.
  Cooking is one of my favorite hobbies.

• after prepositions and phrasal verbs.
  We're thinking of going out for a meal.
  She's looking forward to trying that restaurant.

• after some verbs, including *enjoy, feel like, finish, hate, keep, like, love, (don't) mind, miss, prefer, recommend, spend time, suggest.*
  I love trying new food.
  I prefer cooking at home to eating out.

We put *not* before an -ing form to make a negative.
I love not having to get up early on the weekend.

We use the infinitive with *to*:

• after adjectives.
  It's easy to cook this kind of food.
  It's expensive to eat out in this city.

• after some verbs, including *afford, agree, decide, expect, forget, help, hope, learn, need, offer, plan, promise, refuse, want, hate, like, love, prefer.*
  We decided to go out for coffee.
  Julie offered to cook me dinner.

• to give a reason.
  I went to the supermarket to get some food for the party.

We put *not* before an infinitive to make a negative.
He promised not to make the same mistake again.

> **Look!** We can use the verbs *begin, continue,* and *start* with an -ing form or an infinitive, without any change in meaning.
> *He started running. / He started to run.*
> We can also use the verbs *prefer, hate, like,* and *love* with an -ing form or an infinitive, without any change in meaning.
> *I hate doing homework on weekends. / I hate to do homework on weekends.*

With some verbs, we use an object before the infinitive.
Carl asked her to marry him.
He told Sara to call him.
They want me to go with them.
I would like you to help me with the dinner.
We expect him to pass the exam.

1 Choose the correct options to complete the sentences.

  1 It was hard *to find / find* your house because it doesn't have a number.

  2 Jackie suggested *to go / going* to see a movie tonight.

  3 I offered *to help / helping* my brother with his homework.

  4 We went outside *for getting / to get* some fresh air.

  5 *Live / Living* downtown is very expensive.

  6 I don't mind *getting up / to get up* early in the morning.

  7 I decided to give up *to eat / eating* sugar for a week.

  8 *Growing / To grow* up in the country was great.

  9 I'm tired of *going / to go* to the same restaurant all the time.

  10 I would love *speaking / to speak* English as well as you.

2 Complete the conversation with the correct form of the verb in parentheses.

A Hey, Mike. Do you want ¹_____ (do) something tonight?

B Sure. How about ²_____ (go) to see that new sci-fi movie at the old theater in town?

A But it's so hot today. ³_____ (sit) in a hot movie theater doesn't sound like much fun! I think I'd prefer ⁴_____ (be) outdoors.

B OK, do you feel like ⁵_____ (go) to that concert in the park?

A Great idea. Do you mind ⁶_____ (give) me a lift?

B No, of course not. I'll come get you when I finish ⁷_____ (clean) the kitchen.

A OK, thanks. Don't forget ⁸_____ (bring) my jacket. Remember, I left it in your car last week.

◄ Go back to page 81

10A Reported speech

 10.4

He **said that he knew** where the burglar lived.
The police **told us that they had arrested** someone for the crime.
I **asked Emma if she could** help me with my homework.
The police officer **asked me where I had been** the night before.

We use reported speech to say what someone said.

Direct speech: *"I live downtown."*
Reported speech: *She said (that) she lived downtown.*

In reported speech, we usually change the tense of the verbs:

- simple present → simple past
  "I work in a bank." → *He said (that) he worked in a bank.*
- present continuous → past continuous
  "The train is arriving." → *Sara said (that) the train was arriving.*
- present perfect → past perfect
  "I've finished work." → *Mike told me (that) he'd finished work.*
- simple past → past perfect
  "I lost my keys." → *She said (that) she'd lost her keys.*

Some modal verbs also change in reported speech.

"I can speak French." → *Luke said (that) he could speak French.*
"I'll see you tonight." → *Lisa said (that) she would see us tonight.*
"We may get married." → *Sarah told me (that) they might get married.*
"We have to buy her a present." → *They said (that) they had to buy her a present.*

The following modal verbs don't change in reported speech: *would, could, might,* and *should*.

Reported statements

The most common verbs that we use to report statements are *say* and *tell*. When we use *say*, we don't usually specify the person who was spoken to.

He said that he was Spanish. NOT ~~He said me that he was Spanish.~~

When we use *tell*, we always specify the person who was spoken to.

He told me that he was Spanish. NOT ~~He told that he was Spanish.~~

We often use *that* after *said* and *told* but it isn't essential.

Reported questions

We report a *Yes/No* question with the following structure:

subject + *asked* + (object) + *if* + subject + affirmative verb form + rest of sentence.

"Do you want ice cream?" → *She asked (me) if I wanted ice cream.*
"Is this your car?" → *He asked (me) if it was my car.*

When we report *wh-* questions, we include the question word(s) instead of *if*.

"Why did you call me?" → *She asked (me) why I had called her.*
"When will you buy a car?" → *They asked (us) when we would buy a car.*

Look! In reported speech, we change pronouns and words referring to time and place if the sentence is reported on a different day or in a different place.
"I'm coming tomorrow." → *She said she was coming the next day.*
"We visited him yesterday." → *They said they had visited him the day before.*
"I'll wait for you here." → *He said he'd wait for us there.*

1 Complete the sentences with reported speech.

1 "I'll see you at eight o'clock."
Mike told me _____ at eight o'clock.
2 "I'm seeing Maria this weekend."
She said _____ Maria this weekend.
3 "I've lost my phone."
Martin said _____ phone.
4 "I can't speak Portuguese."
Susan told them _____ Portuguese.
5 "I bought a new car last week."
She told me _____ before.
6 "Do you like going to the movies?"
He asked her _____ going to the movies.
7 "Why didn't you wait for me last night?"
She asked me _____ last night.
8 "Can you buy me this red dress?"
She asked me _____ the red dress.

2 Complete the story. Look at the direct speech below and use reported speech in the story.

"He used his own car to drive to and from the bank."
"He forgot to change his black T-shirt with his name on it."
"Do you recognize the man in this photograph?"
"He's the man who robbed the bank this morning."
"We can't afford to pay the rent for our home any more."
"I didn't tell my wife about the robbery."
"I borrowed the money."

It only took Denver police five hours to find the man who had robbed the Wells Fargo bank. But they had a little help from the robber! Police said that the suspect [1]_____ his own car to drive to and from the bank. They also said that he [2]_____ to change his black T-shirt with his name on it before robbing the bank.

Police soon identified the man from the license plate on the car and printed a photograph of him. When they went to the bank and asked a bank worker [3]_____ the man in the photograph, she said that he [4]_____ the man who [5]_____ the bank that morning. Later they found his car at a hotel nearby and arrested him in his room. The suspect said that he and his wife were staying at the hotel because they [6]_____ afford to pay the rent for their own home any more. He said that he [7]_____ his wife about the robbery. Instead he told her that [8]_____ the money.

◀ Go back to page 85

10C Second conditional, *would*, *could*, and *might*

 10.11

If I **argued** with my best friend, **I'd be** sad.
I'd visit you every year **if you lived** near the coast.
If I **could speak** Spanish, **I'd go** traveling in South America.
If I **won** the lottery, I **might give** all the money to charity.
If I **were** you, **I'd update** my résumé.

We use the second conditional to talk about impossible or very unlikely hypothetical situations in the present or future and their consequences.

Impossible situation

If I were rich, I'd buy a big house by the sea. (I'm not rich, so it's impossible for me to buy a big house by the sea.)

Unlikely situation

If my new phone stopped working tomorrow, I'd take it back to the store. (It's a new phone, so this probably won't happen.)

We form the *if* clause with *if* + simple past, and we form the main clause with *would* + base form. The *if* clause can come either at the beginning or at the end of the sentence with no change in meaning.

If you went to bed earlier, you wouldn't feel so tired.
You wouldn't feel so tired if you went to bed earlier.

We can also use *could* or *might* in the main clause to say that something would be possible.

If we lived by the sea, we could go swimming every day.
If you asked John more politely, he might help you.

With the verb *be*, we often use *were* instead of *was* in the *if* clause with *I*, *he*, *she*, and *it*. We often use *were* in the phrase *If I were you* … to give advice.

If Adam were here, he would fix your computer.
If I were you, I'd take a cab to the airport.

Look! Don't use *would* in the *if* clause.
If I had more time, I'd learn the saxophone. NOT ~~If I would have more time, I'd learn the saxophone.~~

Second conditional or first conditional?

We use the first conditional when we think a future event is likely. We use the second conditional when we think a future event is less likely.

If it rains tomorrow, we'll go shopping. (It often rains here, so it might rain.)
If it rained tomorrow, we'd go shopping. (It probably won't rain.)

---

1 Complete the second conditional sentences with the correct form of the verbs in parentheses.

1 If I _____ (live) downtown, I _____ (walk) to work.
2 This city _____ (be) much nicer if there _____ (be) less traffic on the streets.
3 If you _____ (get up) a bit earlier, you _____ (not be) late for work so often.
4 If we _____ (have) a bigger car, we _____ (can) take more things on vacation with us.
5 What _____ (you/do) if someone _____ (steal) your car?
6 I _____ (play) basketball if I _____ (be) a bit taller.
7 If I _____ (be) you, I _____ (ask) my boss for a promotion.
8 If you _____ (not spend) so much money on clothes, you _____ (be able to) afford a new phone.

2 Complete the second sentences. Use the second conditional to link the situations in the first sentences.

1 I'm lazy. I always get bad grades in school.
   If I wasn't lazy, I wouldn't always get bad grades in school.
2 I have a small bedroom. I don't have enough space for all my books.
   If I _____ , _____ enough space for all my books.
3 It's so hot today. I can't concentrate on my work.
   If _____ , _____ on my work.
4 I don't get any exercise. I'm so out of shape.
   If I _____ , _____ so out of shape.
5 I feel tired. I can't play tennis this afternoon.
   If I _____ , _____ this afternoon.
6 I drink coffee in the evening. I don't sleep well.
   If I _____ , _____ better.

3 Complete the sentences with the correct form of the verbs in parentheses. Use the first or second conditional.

1 If we _____ (leave) now, we'll get there on time.
2 What would you do if you _____ (win) $1,000?
3 If you _____ (have) a car, you could drive to work.
4 _____ (you/go) to college if you get good grades this year?
5 If he _____ (ask) her to marry him, what would she say?
6 We'll play tennis later if it _____ (stop) raining.
7 I _____ (not accept) that job if they offered it to me.
8 If they win, they _____ (be) the champions.

◀ Go back to page 89

11A Articles

 11.3

My best friend is **an architect**.
You're **the funniest** person I know.
They sent him to **prison** for six years.

We go on vacation **three times a year**.
I'm going to **the Czech Republic** soon.
Floods are common in this country.

Indefinite article (*a/an*)

We use *a/an* with singular, countable nouns:

- to talk about something or somebody for the first time.
  Suddenly, a man ran out of the bank.

- to describe something or somebody.
  It's a beautiful building.   She's a really funny person.

- to talk about a person's job.
  He's a computer programmer.   She works as an accountant.

- in frequency and measurement expressions.
  I go to the gym twice a week.   He was driving at over 150 km. an hour.

Definite article (*the*)

We use *the*:

- to talk about something we've already mentioned, or when it's clear which particular thing or person we're talking about.
  I saw a man and a woman looking at a map. The man asked me for help.
  That restaurant looks nice, but the prices are very high. (This clearly means the prices in the restaurant.)

- when we use a defining relative clause to define a noun.
  That's the boy who stole my bike.

- when there's only one of a thing.
  The sun went behind the clouds.   I reserved our hotel on the Internet.

- with superlative adjectives and ordinal numbers (*first, second, third,* etc.).
  She was the first person I met at the party.

- with the names of rivers, seas, oceans, and groups of islands.
  London is on the River Thames.   We're flying over the Pacific Ocean.
  Last year I went to the Galápagos Islands.

- before countries that include the words *United, Republic,* and *Kingdom,* or are plurals.
  I'd love to visit the U.S.

No article (zero article)

We don't use an article:

- to talk about things in general (with plural or uncountable nouns).
  Houses are more expensive than apartments. (houses and apartments in general)
  Sugar is bad for you. (sugar in general, and not the sugar in this packet)

- with some places where we work, live, study, or do other specific activities, such as *work, school, college, prison, church*. We usually use them with no article after a preposition.
  I stayed (at) home all day.   Chris is in college in Boston.

- before *next/last* + *day, week, month, year,* etc.
  I saw him last week.   We'd like to stay in the same hotel next July.

- with most names of streets, towns, cities, countries, and continents.
  He lives on Pine Street.   We're going to New York next week!
  I hope to visit Australia one day.

1 Choose the correct options to complete the sentences.

  1 That was *the / –* best movie I've ever seen!
  2 I go running three times *a / the* week.
  3 I have to go to *– / the* work now. I'll call you later.
  4 Look at *a / the* moon – it's really bright tonight.
  5 **A** What do you do?   **B** I'm *a / –* student.
  6 I don't like *the / –* rock music.
  7 The president arrives in *the / –* France on Monday.
  8 Most people now use *– / the* smartphones.
  9 There was *a / –* man selling ice cream outside.
  10 I hope to see you *the / –* next week.

2 Complete the sentences. Add *the* or leave a blank (no article).

  1 _____ food in this restaurant is amazing!
  2 _____ basketball is one of _____ most popular sports in _____ world.
  3 In _____ U.S., _____ tornadoes are pretty common in the Midwest.
  4 _____ girl who gave me those flowers was about ten years old.
  5 I'd like to talk to _____ manager of _____ hotel, please.
  6 _____ boys are usually taller than _____ girls.
  7 I often listen to _____ music while I'm studying.
  8 _____ hotel where I stayed had a beautiful view of _____ sea.

3 Complete the text. Add *a, an,* or *the* or leave a blank (no article).

I think that [1]_____ most beautiful place to visit in Colombia is Tayrona National Park. It's [2]_____ protected area on [3]_____ Caribbean coast, 34 kilometers from [4]_____ city of Santa Marta. There's [5]_____ amazing rainforest in [6]_____ park where you might see [7]_____ monkeys, parrots, frogs, and iguanas. I went to a magnificent beach at Cabo San Juan, which was [8]_____ perfect place to swim and to watch [9]_____ spectacular sunset over [10]_____ sea. [11]_____ tourists love going to Tayrona National Park, so if you want to avoid the crowds, [12]_____ quietest time to visit [13]_____ park is during [14]_____ off season, from February to November.

◀ Go back to page 95

11C Third conditional

 11.6

If Emil **hadn't** stayed out all night, his parents **wouldn't have been** so furious.
I would **have come** to the party if I**'d known** about it.
If I**'d studied** more before my exam, I **might have passed**.
If you**'d called** me earlier, we **could have gone** out for dinner.

We use the third conditional to talk about hypothetical (unreal) situations in the past and their consequences.

If I'd seen your e-mail, I would have replied to it. (I didn't see your e-mail. I didn't reply to it.)

If he'd taken a cab, he wouldn't have missed his train. (He didn't take a cab. He missed his train.)

We form the *if* clause with *if* + past perfect. We form the main clause with *would have* + past participle.

If you had come with us, you would have had a great time.
If the bus hadn't been late, we would have arrived at the theater before the movie started.

The *if* clause can come either at the beginning or at the end of the sentence with no change in meaning.

If it had been sunny yesterday, we would have gone for a walk.
We would have gone for a walk if it had been sunny yesterday.

We can use *might* or *may* instead of *would* when the consequences weren't certain.

If I hadn't arrived late to the interview, I might have gotten the job.
If they'd stayed longer at the beach, we may have seen them.

We can use *could* instead of *would* to talk about hypothetical possibilities.

If my car hadn't broken down, I could have taken you to the airport yesterday.
If they'd told us about the problem, we could have helped them.

Look! The contraction *'d* can mean *had* or *would* although we often don't contract would in the third conditional..
If I'd (I had) known you were in the hospital, I'd (I would) have come to visit you.

1 Complete the sentences with the correct form of the verbs in parentheses to make third conditional sentences.

1 If you _____ (ask) me for some money, I _____ (give) it to you.
2 We _____ (not stay) at that hotel if you _____ (not recommend) it.
3 I _____ (go) to the party if they _____ (invite) me.
4 If they _____ (arrive) five minutes earlier, they _____ (not miss) the flight.
5 If you _____ (not drive) so slowly, we _____ (arrive) home an hour ago.
6 I _____ (go) to the concert last Saturday if I _____ (know) it was free.
7 If you _____ (take) a better map, you _____ (not get) lost.
8 We _____ (not go) to the beach yesterday if we _____ (see) the weather forecast.

2 Write sentences about how these situations and consequences in the past would have been different. Use the third conditional.

1 You didn't work hard last year. You didn't pass your exams.
If you had worked hard last year, you would have passed your exams.
2 There was a lot of traffic. We arrived late for the meeting.
_____
3 She cut her finger badly. I took her to the hospital.
_____
4 It was really hot yesterday. We didn't play tennis.
_____
5 I left my phone at home. I couldn't call you.
_____
6 I didn't know it was your birthday today. I didn't buy you a present.
_____
7 He trained hard every day. He won the race.
_____
8 You didn't stop at the red light. The police officer gave you a fine.

◀ Go back to page 99

12A *So/Neither do I*

> ▶ **12.3**
>
> "I love playing golf." "**So do I.**"
> "I'd love to visit New Zealand one day." "**So would I.**"
> "I'm not very good at chess." "**Neither am I.**"
> "I couldn't go to class last week." "**Neither could I.**"
> "I haven't done my homework." "**Really? I have.**"
> "I'm going on vacation next month." "**I'm not.**"

Agreeing

When we want to show that we agree with someone, or what he or she says is the same for us, we can use *so* or *neither* instead of repeating the whole sentence.

I can ski pretty well.
So can I. (= I can ski pretty well.)

I don't like rap music.
Neither do I. (= I don't like rap music.)

We use *so* to agree with an affirmative statement, and we use *neither* to agree with a negative statement. These are both followed by the auxiliary or modal verb from the first statement + *I*.

I'm at the airport.	*So am I.*
I can speak Spanish.	*So can I.*
I've never been abroad.	*Neither have I.*
I won't be late.	*Neither will I.*

If the statement is in the simple present or simple past, we use the auxiliary *do/does* or *did* to agree with the other person.

I live near the sea.	*So do I.*
I didn't like the hotel.	*Neither did I.*

Disagreeing

When something that someone says isn't true for us, or what is said is different for us, we can use *I* + auxiliary or modal verb from the first statement. We often respond with *Really* first.

I don't like traveling by train.	*Really? I do.*
I've never tried mint ice cream.	*Really? I have. It's delicious!*

After an affirmative statement that isn't the same for us, we use *I* + negative auxiliary or modal verb, such as *I'm not.* / *I don't.* / *I didn't.* / *I can't.* / *I wouldn't.*

I really enjoyed that movie.	*I didn't.*
I love going running after work.	*I don't. I hate running.*

After a negative statement that isn't the same for us, we use an affirmative auxiliary or modal verb.

I didn't enjoy that movie.	*Really? I did.*
I can't help Leo with his homework.	*I can. Don't worry.*

1 Complete the replies with the words in the box.

> could   did (x2)   so   would
> can   neither   have   do   'm not

1 A I love sightseeing.
   B So _____ I. It's better than lying on the beach.
2 A I've never been to Japan.
   B Neither _____ I. But I'd like to go one day.
3 A I can't swim very well.
   B Oh, I _____ . I'm a very good swimmer.
4 A I'm staying at home tonight.
   B Really? I _____ . I'm going out.
5 A I didn't like that movie.
   B _____ did I. I thought it was really boring.
6 A I'd love to go to New York one day.
   B Yes, _____ would I.
7 A I just bought a new camera.
   B So _____ I. What a coincidence!
8 A I didn't buy her a present for her birthday.
   B Neither _____ I.
9 A I'd like to watch that new reality show.
   B Yes, so _____ I.
10 A Unfortunately, I couldn't go to her party.
   B No, neither _____ I.

2 Write replies to agree (✔) or disagree (✗) with the statements. Use *so* or *neither* or *I* + auxiliary or modal.

1 I've finished all my homework. (✔)
   So have I.
2 I won't go to bed late tonight.
   _____ . (✔)
3 I like going to the movies by myself.
   _____ . (✗)
4 I can't speak French very well.
   _____ . (✔)
5 I usually drive to work.
   _____ . (✔)
6 I'm going to the U.S. in the summer.
   _____ . (✔)
7 I'm not going to Luke's party.
   _____ . (✗)
8 I haven't bought my ticket yet.
   _____ . (✔)
9 I didn't enjoy reading that book.
   _____ . (✗)
10 I'd love to see her again.
   _____ . (✔)

◀ Go back to page 103

12C Modals of deduction

 12.11

I can't hear the children. They **must be** in bed.
I haven't seen Lukas for a few days. He **might be** on vacation.
You **might not like** this new café. They only serve coffee, not tea.
Sandra's not at work today. She **may be** sick.
It's very noisy in the apartment upstairs. They **must be having** a party.

We use modals of deduction to talk about something when we don't know if it's definitely true.

We use *must* + base form when we think that something is true.

It must be cold outside. Everyone's wearing gloves. (= I'm sure it's cold outside.)

We use *can't* or *couldn't* + base form when we are sure that something isn't true.

Sally can't live here. This is a house, and she said she lived in an apartment. (= I'm sure that Sally doesn't live here.)

We use *might* or *might not* + base form when we think it's possible that something is true, but we're not sure.

Mark isn't answering his phone. He might be in a meeting. Or he might not have it with him. (= It's possible that Mark is in a meeting. It's possible that he doesn't have his phone with him.)

We also use *may* or *could* + base form when we think something is possible.

They're speaking English, so they may be British.
I don't know where he is. He could be at a friend's house.

We often use the continuous form of the verb after modals of deduction when we talk about what we think is happening now.

Tom's not in the kitchen. He must be doing his homework in his bedroom.
They can't be playing soccer now – it's nearly midnight!
She might be talking to David on the phone. He left a message for her this morning.

> **Look!** We never use *can* or contract *must not* to talk about what we think is true. The word *mustn't* has a different meaning and expresses prohibition in British English.
> *Lisa has ordered tofu. She might/could be a vegetarian.* NOT ~~She can be a vegetarian.~~
> *That must not be Steve's coat. It looks too small.* NOT ~~That mustn't be Steve's coat. It looks too small.~~

1 Choose the correct options to complete the sentences.

1 John didn't sleep at all last night. He *must / can't* be really tired today.
2 Where's Lidia? She *can't / might* be at work because her office is closed today.
3 Let's try that store over there. It *might / can* be cheaper, but I'm not sure.
4 We *can / can't* be at the right address. There's no restaurant here.
5 A Is Vicki's husband from Australia?
   B I think he *might / can't* be, but I've never asked him.
6 I never see Max studying, so he *can't / must* be a very good student.
7 Look, Brian *must / can* be home – the lights are on in his apartment.
8 This *must / may* be the museum Lucy was talking about. I'm absolutely sure.
9 That movie won three Oscars, so it *can't / must* be good.
10 The people on the street have opened their umbrellas so it *can't / must* be raining.

2 Complete the second sentences so they mean the same as the first sentences. Use *must*, *might*, or *can't*.

1 Luke's not here. <u>It's possible</u> that he's sick.
   Luke's not here. He _____ sick.
2 <u>I'm sure</u> that's not Martin's car. His is much bigger.
   That _____ Martin's car. His is much bigger.
3 Steve goes to the pool every day at this time. <u>He's definitely</u> swimming right now.
   Steve _____ swimming right now – he goes to the pool every day at this time.
4 <u>It's possible</u> that there are still tickets available for the concert.
   There _____ tickets available for the concert.
5 <u>It seems impossible</u> that this dish is very healthy – it's full of sugar.
   This dish _____ very healthy – it's full of sugar.
6 <u>I'm totally sure</u> she knows Toni – I saw them talking at the party.
   She _____ Toni – I saw them talking at the party.
7 <u>It's possible</u> that they're waiting for us outside.
   They _____ for us outside.
8 <u>I don't believe</u> that it's snowing. It's the middle of May!
   It _____ . It's the middle of May!

◀ Go back to page 107

7A   Movies

1 ▶ **7.1** Match the words and phrases in the box with definitions 1–10. Listen and check.

> scene   sequel   director   cast   subtitles   soundtrack   special effects   plot   script   main character

1 the people who act in a movie _____
2 the person who makes a movie _____
3 the story of the movie _____
4 a movie that continues the story of another movie _____
5 words written at the bottom of the screen _____

6 a short section of a movie _____
7 the spoken words of the movie _____
8 the music of the movie _____
9 images that are usually created by computer _____
10 the most important person in the movie's story _____

2 A ▶ **7.2** Match the phrases in **bold** in the text with sentences a–g.

Blade Runner is one of the most famous science fiction movies ever made. [1]It was <u>directed by</u> Ridley Scott, and [2]the main character was <u>played by</u> Harrison Ford. [3]The movie is <u>set in</u> Los Angeles in the year 2019, and [4]it was <u>shot</u> at the Warner Brothers' studio in Hollywood and on location in L.A. The movie is about a police officer who is trying to find a group of dangerous androids. [5]It's <u>based on</u> a novel called *Do Androids Dream of Electric Sheep?* by Philip K Dick. When [6]*Blade Runner* was <u>released</u> in 1982, not all of the movie critics liked it, but these days it's a science fiction classic. [7]It has been <u>dubbed</u> into a lot of different languages, and its sequel, *Blade Runner 2049*, was released in 2017. It stars Harrison Ford, Ryan Gosling, and Ana de Armas.

a The story happens in this place and at this time. _____
b This book inspired the story in the movie. _____
c It was filmed in this place. _____
d This person was the movie director. _____

e The movie was shown in theaters for the first time. _____
f This actor had this role in the movie. _____
g The original spoken words of the movie have been replaced with words in another language. _____

B Look at the <u>underlined</u> words in 2A. Listen and repeat.

3 ▶ **7.3** Match the types of movies in the box with definitions 1–8. Listen and check.

> action movie   animation   horror movie   romantic comedy   science-fiction movie   thriller   musical   documentary

1 an exciting movie, often with a plot about solving a crime _____
2 a movie set in the future, often about space travel _____
3 a movie with a plot about an amusing love story _____
4 a movie that gives facts and information about something _____
5 a lot of the story is told using songs in this type of movie _____
6 a frightening movie, often about killers, dead people, or monsters _____
7 a movie that often has a hero who fights or chases bad people _____
8 a movie of moving images made by using drawings or models _____

> **Look!** We shorten the forms of some movie types.
> *I love sci-fi movies.*

7C TV and music

1 ▶ **7.7** Match the types of TV shows in the box with pictures 1–9. Listen and check.

> game show   talk show   drama   reality show   cartoon   sitcom   soap opera   the news   talent show

1 _____

2 _____

3 _____

4 _____

5 _____

6 _____

7 _____

8 _____

9 _____

2 ▶ **7.8** Complete sentences 1–6 with the words in the box. Listen and check.

> ads   audience   channel   episode   host   series   season

1 Can you change the _____, please? The news is on at 9:00 p.m., and I want to watch it.

2 I'm going to make coffee while the _____ are on, so I don't miss the show.

3 Everyone in the _____ laughed when the host told a joke about the politician.

4 I prefer watching TV _____ to movies. My favorite is *Game of Thrones*. _____ one was the best!

5 I can't stand this _____ . He always asks his guests such silly questions.

6 I missed the last _____ of that soap opera. What happened?

3 ▶ **7.9** Complete sentences 1–7 with the words in the box. Listen and check.

> band   tracks   playlist   on tour   hits   live (adj.)   album

1 My favorite _____ is *The Best of Jana* by a singer called Jana.

2 Why don't you choose your favorite 50 songs and make a _____ for the party?

3 When I saw Shakira in concert last year, she sang all of her _____ , including my favorite song, *Whenever, Wherever*.

4 When we were students, my sister and I were in a _____ . I was the singer, and she played the guitar.

5 I love seeing my favorite groups _____ in concert.

6 I can't wait for my favorite singer to go _____ . I hope she plays at the stadium in my city.

7 There are 20 _____ on that album.

◀ Go back to page 62

147

8A Sports, places, and equipment

1 ▶ 8.2 Match the words in the box with pictures 1–9.
Listen and check.

> ball bat skates goal net goggles racket stick helmet

1 _____ 2 _____ 3 _____

4 _____ 5 _____ 6 _____ 7 _____ 8 _____ 9 _____

2 ▶ 8.3 Match the sports with pictures 1–12. Listen and check.

> soccer diving basketball hockey ice skating track and field auto racing baseball swimming volleyball tennis football

1 _____ 2 _____ 3 _____ 4 _____

5 _____ 6 _____ 7 _____ 8 _____

9 _____ 10 _____ 11 _____ 12 _____

3 A ▶ 8.4 Look at words 1–6 in 3B. Listen and repeat.

B Match the sports in exercise 2 with the places.

1 court _____ _____   3 rink _____ _____   5 circuit _____
2 field _____ _____   4 pool _____ _____   6 track _____

◀ Go back to page 66

8B Health and fitness verb phrases

1 ▶ 8.9 Complete the text with the correct form of *get*, *be*, or *have*. Listen and check.

Do you ¹_____ **an unhealthy lifestyle**?
It's very easy these days to ²_____ **bad habits** when it comes to exercise, food, and sleep. If you'd like to ³_____ **a healthy lifestyle**, talk to your doctor and follow the advice below.

- Try to ⁴_____ **exercise** five times a week for at least 30 minutes. Adults need 150 minutes of moderate aerobic activity every week, or 75 minutes of vigorous activity.
- Make sure you ⁵_____ **a balanced diet**. Eat a variety of foods from all five food groups, but limit how much sugar, fat, and salt you eat.
- Even in stressful situations, try not to ⁶_____ **stressed**. Make sure you have enough time to relax. Regular exercise helps reduce stress levels.

- Exercise also helps you lose weight if you ⁷_____ **overweight**, and if you are out of shape, it helps you to ⁸_____ **in shape**.
- If you ⁹_____ **on a diet**, don't try to lose weight too quickly.
- If you ¹⁰_____ **underweight**, aim to eat food that is high in energy, for example, peanut butter on toast or a baked potato with tuna.
- It's important to ¹¹_____ **a good night's sleep**. We all need different amounts of sleep, but most adults need 7–9 hours a night.

2 Complete the sentences with the correct form of the verb phrases in exercise 1.

1 There's a lot of pressure on my job. I often _____ out.
2 My grandmother _____ . She plays tennis regularly and eats healthy food.
3 I try to _____ by eating lots of different foods, especially vegetables, fruit, meat, and fish.
4 I _____ four times a week. I usually go to the gym or go running.

5 Jack was sick for a month and didn't eat much. Now he _____ and has to eat a lot of protein.
6 I have a three-month-old baby who wakes me up every hour, so it's difficult to _____ .
7 No chocolate cake for me, thanks. I _____ . I can only eat low-fat food.

◀ Go back to page 68

10B Making nouns from verbs

1 ▶ 10.6 Make nouns from the verbs in the box below and write them in the chart on the right. Listen and check.

-sion	-ment	-ation	-tion
confusion			

confuse argue imagine govern inform protect achieve
connect disappoint decide educate organize

2 Complete the second sentences with a noun so they have the same meaning as the first sentences.

1 Antivirus software protects computers from viruses.
Antivirus software offers computers _____ from viruses.
2 Thanks to Sarah for organizing the event so well.
Thanks to Sarah for your great _____ .
3 A lot was achieved in the twentieth century. Walking on the moon is one of the best examples of this.
Walking on the moon was one of the best _____ of the twentieth century.
4 Educating our children is a huge responsibility.
Our children's _____ is a huge responsibility.
5 A large city has to govern effectively. A large city has to have an effective _____ .

6 I went to a concert last week, but I was disappointed.
The concert I went to last week was a _____ .
7 Last night my neighbors were arguing really loudly.
Last night my neighbors were having a really loud _____ .
8 We decided to sell our car and use public transportation instead.
We made the _____ to sell our car and use public transportation instead.
9 The lesson was very difficult, so a lot of people were confused.
There was a lot of _____ because the lesson was very difficult.
10 Nobody informed us why the flight had been canceled.
We didn't receive any _____ about why the flight had been canceled.

◀ Go back to page 86

9A   Food and cooking

1   ▶ **9.1** Match the foods in the box with pictures 1–11. Listen and check.

chickpeas   steak   lime   yogurt   lentils   asparagus   lamb chop   lobster   squid   skim milk   whole wheat bread

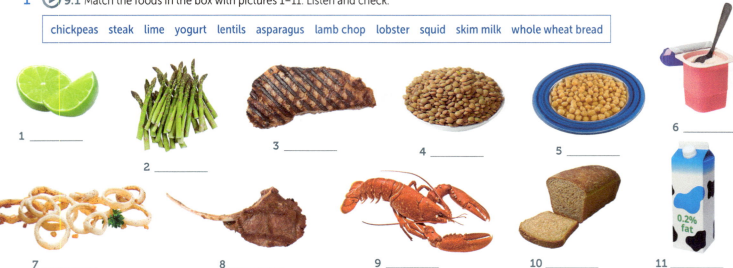

1 _____

2 _____

3 _____

4 _____

5 _____

6 _____

7 _____

8 _____

9 _____

10 _____

11 _____

2 A ▶ **9.2** Put the words in the box in the correct column of the chart. Add the words from exercise 1. Listen and check.

B Add other food words you know to the chart.

zucchini   olive oil   garlic   soy sauce   toast   shellfish   avocado

seafood	meat	dairy products	legumes	fruit and vegetables	carbohydrates	other
		yogurt	*lentils*			

3   ▶ **9.3** Look at the pictures. Complete descriptions 1–10 with the words in the box. Listen and check.

baked   boiled   grated   grilled   homemade   melted   roast   sliced   takeout   fried

1 _____ egg

2 _____ potato

3 _____ burger

4 _____ beef

5 _____ chicken

6 _____ rice

7 _____ cheese

8 _____ carrot

9 _____ food

10 _____ soup

◀ Go back to page 76

9C Eating out

1 A Read the conversations. Match the phrases in **bold** with definitions a–j.

A Should we ¹**eat out** tonight or get some takeout?
B Let's eat out. I'll ²**reserve a table** at that new place on Main Street.
A Great! I've heard that the food is delicious, and there's a nice ³**atmosphere**, too – it's relaxed, welcoming, and they have good music.
B I hope the ⁴**service** is good, too. I hate rude waiters.

A I'll have the steak.
B How would you like your steak? ⁵**Rare**? ⁶**Medium**?
A ⁷**Well-done**, please.

A I'm still hungry! Let's ⁸**order** dessert.
B No, I'm tired. Can we just ⁹**get the check**?
A Sure. Do you have any cash so we can ¹⁰**leave a tip**?

a make a reservation for a particular time ____
b when meat is cooked a lot ____
c eat at a restaurant ____
d ask how much the meal is so you can pay ____
e when meat is cooked a little, and it's still red ____

f tell the waiter what you want to eat ____
g the feeling inside the restaurant ____
h when meat is cooked more than a little, but not a lot ____
i how the staff treats the customers ____
j leave a small amount of money for the waiter ____

B ▶ 9.7 Look at the words and phrases in **bold** in 1A. Listen and repeat.

2 ▶ 9.8 Look at the pictures. Match objects 1–10 with words in the box. Listen and check.

napkin   vinegar   knife   fork   spoon   plate   salt   pepper   bowl   tablecloth

1 _____
2 _____
3 _____
4 _____
5 _____

6 _____
7 _____
8 _____
9 _____
10 _____

10A Crime

1 A Match sentences 1–8 with pictures a–h.

1 The police stopped me because I was driving too fast. I had to pay a $200 _____.

2 A _____ saw a masked man running away from the bank with a bag full of money. Police officers _____ the robber moments later.

3 The _____ was found dead on the dining-room floor.

4 In most countries, it's against the _____ to drive while holding a cell phone.

5 They're building a new _____ in my town with space for 500 criminals.

6 The police aren't sure who committed the crime, but they have released pictures of two _____ .

7 My neighbor's son is appearing in _____ . The police say he stole $75,000.

8 If you leave valuable objects in your car on this street, someone will _____ it and steal them.

B ▶ **10.1** Complete the sentences in exercise 1A with the correct form of the words in the box below. Listen and check.

> arrest   break into   court   fine   law   prison   suspects   victim   witness

2 ▶ **10.2** Match the descriptions of crimes 1–5 with the words in the box below. Listen and check.

> theft   murder   robbery   mugging   burglary

1 Two people entered a house at night through an open window. They took jewelry and two computers. _____

2 A man attacked me on the street. He made me give him my phone and all my money. _____

3 He walked into the house and killed the man inside. _____

4 Three armed men ran into the bank and told the staff to give them all the money. _____

5 I left my bike at the train station. When I went back, it wasn't there. _____

3 ▶ **10.3** Complete the chart below with the words in the box. Listen and check.

> robber   burglarize   murderer   thief   mug
> rob   steal   mugger   murder   burglar

crime	verb	criminal
theft		
murder		
robbery		
mugging		
burglary		

HAVE YOU SEEN THESE PEOPLE?   POLICE

BANK

◀ Go back to page 84

11A The natural world

1 ▶ 11.1 Match the words in the box with pictures 1–11. Listen and check.

sea canyon hill iceberg coast desert field forest glacier jungle volcano

1 _____

2 _____

3 _____

4 _____

5 _____

6 _____

7 _____

8 _____

9 _____

10 _____

11 _____

2 ▶ 11.2 Match the words in the box with descriptions 1–8. Listen and check.

earthquake flood hail hurricane monsoon rainbow storm tornado

1 an arc of colors in the sky _____

2 strong winds with rain, thunder, and lightning _____

3 a very strong wind that can destroy towns _____

4 when an area of normally dry land is covered with water _____

5 when the ground shakes violently _____

6 a very strong wind that moves in a circle and can lift cars and houses _____

7 a season of heavy summer rain in some tropical regions _____

8 small, hard balls of ice that fall from the sky _____

◀ Go back to page 94

11C Extreme adjectives

1 ▶ 11.5 Read sentences 1–12 and match the extreme adjectives in **bold** to adjectives a–l. Listen and check.

1 It's **boiling** in here. Can I open a window? ____
2 Liam gave me an **enormous** bunch of flowers. I needed three vases for them! ____
3 After running the marathon, the athlete looked absolutely **exhausted**! ____
4 I've been playing soccer in the mud. My clothes are **filthy**. ____
5 Put on a scarf, hat, and gloves – it's **freezing** outside! ____
6 He was **furious** when his neighbor crashed into his car. ____
7 He tells **hilarious** jokes. He's an absolutely fantastic comedian! ____
8 He looked so **miserable** when the other team scored the winning goal. ____
9 I haven't eaten all day – I'm absolutely **starving**. ____
10 He was riding a **tiny** bike. He was much too big for it. ____
11 Your back yard is **gorgeous**! You must be really proud of it. ____
12 Lena is a **fantastic** violinist. I'm sure she'll play professionally one day. ____

a very hungry
b very sad
c very small
d very tired
e very good
f very cold
g very big
h very pretty
i very hot
j very angry
k very dirty
l very funny

2 Complete the sentences with an extreme adjective from exercise 1.

1 Simon's just bought an _____ house – it has six bedrooms!
2 I'm _____ because I didn't have time to have lunch today.
3 Sara's feeling _____ because she failed all her exams.
4 You haven't washed your car for ages – it's absolutely _____ !
5 I worked from 7 a.m. to 8 p.m. today, so now I'm _____ !
6 It was snowing and absolutely _____ when we arrived in Moscow last night.
7 My grandfather was _____ when he saw that the boys had broken his window.
8 They didn't have any air conditioning, so it was absolutely _____ .
9 Paul's new girlfriend is _____ . I think she's a model.
10 He has a _____ apartment. It only has one room, plus a little kitchen and bathroom.
11 We just came back from seeing a _____ movie at the theater – we couldn't stop laughing.
12 I just finished reading a _____ book. It's the best book I've read in years!

◀ Go back to page 98

12A Phrases with *go* and *get*

1 A Match the words in the box with *go* phrases 1–4.

> a guided tour traveling coffee school a trip bed a walk
> away hiking scuba diving vacation home college

1 go _____ _____ _____ _____ _____
2 go to _____ _____ _____
3 go for _____ _____
4 go on _____ _____ _____

B ▶ 12.1 Listen and repeat the phrases in 1A.

2 Match the use of *get* in each sentence below with meanings a–e.

1 Can you get my glasses? They're in the kitchen. ____
2 We spent all day on the beach, and I got bored. ____
3 Chris got our flights online. ____
4 Did you get my e-mail? ____
5 If we don't leave soon, we won't get there on time. ____

a buy
b arrive
c become
d receive
e bring

3 Choose the correct words to complete sentences 1–6.

1 Simon's going *for / on* a business trip to Tokyo.
2 There are a lot of tourists in the summer. It *gets / goes* really crowded.
3 When we get *at / to* Buenos Aires, Silvia's going to meet us at the airport.
4 When I was in Switzerland, we *went / got* hiking in the mountains.
5 We climbed a mountain, and I *went / got* tired quickly.
6 On our first day in Sydney, we went *to / on* a guided tour.

4 Rewrite the underlined parts of sentences 1–5 with a phrase with *go* or *get*.

1 Would you like to drink coffee with me later? _____
2 It becomes very cold here in winter. _____
3 I'll arrive at your house at about ten o'clock. _____
4 I'd love to visit lots of different places around the world for a year. _____
5 I need to buy some more sun cream. _____

◀ Go back to page 102

12B Air travel

1 ▶ 12.5 Complete the instructions with the correct form of the words and phrases in the box below. Listen and check.

flight attendant   book a flight   pack   check in   window seat   go through security   departure lounge   land   departure board   take off   show your passport   carry-on bag   gate   checked baggage   boarding pass   aisle seat

Booking and flying with Go There Airline

GO THERE AIRLINE

a

On our website you can ¹_____ up to eleven months before the date of travel, and you can ²_____ online for your flight 24 hours before departure time.

b

Make sure you ³_____ your own bags and suitcases. Don't take any prohibited items.

c

You're allowed 20 kg. of ⁴_____ , and you can bring one ⁵_____ with you on the plane. Don't forget to bring valid identification! You'll have to ⁶_____ or identity card.

d

Sometimes there are long lines to ⁷_____ , so make sure you arrive at the airport at least two hours before your flight.

e

Wait for your flight in the ⁸_____ , where you can get coffee. Don't forget to look at the ⁹_____ to see which ¹⁰_____ your flight leaves from.

f

When your flight is called, show your ¹¹_____ to the ¹²_____ , and check your seat number. Do you have an ¹³_____ or a window seat?

g

When you board the plane, find your seat quickly. Fasten your seat belt before the plane ¹⁴_____ . If you have a ¹⁵_____ , enjoy the view!

h

Ninety-five percent of our flights ¹⁶_____ smoothly and on time. That's one more reason to fly with Go There Airline!

2 Match definitions 1–8 with words and phrases from exercise 1.

1 bags you carry on a plane _____
2 when the plane leaves the ground _____
3 the document you show to get on a flight _____
4 preparing your bags before you fly _____
5 a person who works on a plane _____
6 when the plane returns to the ground _____
7 bags you don't carry on a plane _____
8 buy your tickets to fly _____

◀ Go back to page 104

7A Student A

1 Ask Student B the trivia questions using the passive in the correct tense. The correct answer is in **bold**.

1 Which sport / play / at Wimbledon in England?
   a **tennis**
   b soccer
   c cricket

2 How many *Harry Potter* movies / make?
   a five
   b **eight**
   c ten

3 What / invent / by Guglielmo Marconi?
   a the television
   b **the radio**
   c the Internet

4 When / The Taj Mahal in India / build?
   a in the 15th century
   b **in the 17th century**
   c in the 19th century

5 Which animals / can / find / on the flag of Bolivia?
   a **an alpaca and a condor**
   b a lion and a swan
   c an owl and a bear

2 Look at the pictures and listen to Student B's questions. Choose the correct answer a–c.

   a 1789
   b 1889
   c 1989

   a plants
   b life
   c water

   a Istanbul
   b Moscow
   c Athens

   a around 20
   b around 200
   c around 2000

   a the Great Pyramids at Giza
   b the Pentagon
   c the Great Wall of China

7C Student A

1 Ask Student B questions 1–5 using the correct form of *can*, *could*, or *be able to*.

1 _____ you sing well when you were eight years old?
2 Would you like to _____ fly?
3 _____ you watch shows online on your TV?
4 _____ you understand the lyrics of pop songs in English when you were fifteen?
5 Would you like to _____ sing like a famous singer? Who?

2 Answer Student B's questions. Give more information about each answer.

7D Student A

1 Student B is a tourist who is lost. You know the town well. Respond to Student B's questions and give directions using the information in the box.

The museum. 10 minutes away on foot. Follow this street until you get to the traffic light. Take a right, and the museum is about 400 m. down that street on the left. It's next to a pizza restaurant.

2 You are in another town and you're lost. Ask Student B for directions to the train station using prompts 1–5.

1 Ask for help politely.
2 Ask for directions to the train station.
3 Ask if it was right or left at the traffic circle.
4 Repeat the route and ask for confirmation.
5 Thank him/her politely.

8A Student A

1 Look at the chart. You think the facts about James Rodríguez are correct but you're not 100% sure. Use statements with tag questions to check the facts with Student B.

2 Look at the facts about Fabiana Claudino in the chart. Student B will check these facts with you. Correct Student B's facts if necessary.

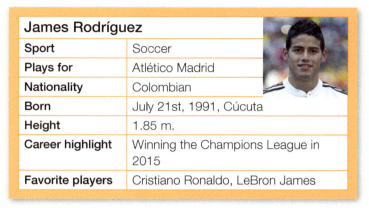

James Rodríguez	
Sport	Soccer
Plays for	Atlético Madrid
Nationality	Colombian
Born	July 21st, 1991, Cúcuta
Height	1.85 m.
Career highlight	Winning the Champions League in 2015
Favorite players	Cristiano Ronaldo, LeBron James

Fabiana Claudino	
Sport	Volleyball
Nationality	Brazilian
Born	January 24th, 1985
Home city	Belo Horizonte
Height	1.93 m.
Career highlight	Winning gold in the 2012 Olympic Games
Favorite type of movie	Action movies

8C Student A

1 Read sentences 1–5 to Student B. Listen to his/her replies. Correct the responses if necessary.

1 Don't forget it's your mom's birthday on Saturday.
Response: You're right. I have to buy her some flowers.
2 When do I need to be at the airport?
Response: You have to be there two hours before the flight.
3 Should I give this banana to the monkey?
Response: No! You can't feed the animals in the zoo.
4 It's 6:30. It's time for me to get up!
Response: You don't have to get up early today. It's Saturday.
5 Do you have a job interview at eight o'clock tomorrow morning?
Response: Yes, I do. I have to go to bed early tonight.

2 Listen to Student B. Respond using a sentence part 1–5 in column 1 and an ending a–e from column 2.

1 I know. I have to	a use your camera in the museum.
2 We don't have to	b change in Miami.
3 No. You can't	c dress up in my office.
4 No, it's not. You have to	d start going to the gym again.
5 Thanks, but you don't have to.	e I can walk.

9A Student A

1 Ask Student B questions 1–6. Student B will respond. Does the response make sense?

1 Do you like spicy food?
2 What do you feel like doing this weekend?
3 Have you ever tried kangaroo meat?
4 What was the new *Batman* movie like?
5 Hi, Jo. I'm calling you from California!
6 Would you like some more pasta?

2 Listen to Student B's questions. Choose the correct response a–f.

a Just a glass of water, please.
b Really? What was it like?
c Not really. I feel like staying in.
d She's really funny.
e He's tall, with dark hair.
f Yes, I love it.

9C Student A

1   Read sentence parts 1–6 to Student B. He/She will complete them. Decide together if the completed sentences make sense.

1   My sister is very good at …
2   It will be very easy for Lisa …
3   My parents really enjoy …
4   My friends and I want …
5   Sam's really worried about …
6   My colleague promised …

2   Listen to Student B. Complete each sentence part with an ending a–f. Decide together if the completed sentences make sense.

a   … to see her old friend Luke tonight.
b   … trying a new Japanese restaurant he heard about.
c   … get a new car at the moment.
d   … to try that new café by the river.
e   … getting a new cell phone next month.
f   … seeing her old friends from school.

9D Student A

1   You and Student B are going to order some takeout. Look at the menu and follow the instructions.

1   Suggest two dishes to share.
2   Listen to Student B.
3   Respond positively to one of his/her suggestions, but not the other. Try to persuade him/her to change his/her mind.
4   If necessary, agree to disagree and choose a third dish.

MIMI's takeout menu

Vegetable lasagna	$10.25
Spicy chicken in coconut milk	$11.50
Lamb, mushroom, and spinach stew	$14
Oven-baked zucchini, eggplant, and potato	$10
Spicy beef burger, salad, and French fries	$12.50
Thai green curry with eggplant and mixed peppers	$9

10A Student A

1   Look at the story. Take turns with Student B and report what the people said. Listen to Student B and complete the missing dialogue.

a   I've lost my phone. Can I borrow yours?

b

c   What does he look like?
He has a beard. He's wearing sunglasses.

d

e   I can hear a phone!

f

2   Check your story with Student B. Do you have the same dialogue?

10C Student A

1 Ask Student B questions 1–4.

1 If you hit another car in a parking lot, would you …
   a leave a note with your name on it to say you're sorry?
   b wait for the owner and pay for the repairs?
   c drive away, hoping that nobody saw you?

2 If you saw somebody stealing food in a supermarket, would you …
   a tell the manager?
   b say nothing?
   c tell the person to stop?

3 If there was an important game on TV while you were still at work, would you …
   a continue working and not think about it?
   b leave work a bit early so you could watch part of it?
   c tell your boss you're sick and watch it at home?

4 If you found the answers to an important exam, would you …
   a give them to your teacher immediately?
   b study them carefully, but get a few of the answers wrong on purpose?
   c study them carefully and get all of the answers right?

2 Listen and answer Student B's questions. Explain your decisions.

11A Student A

1 Read facts 1–5 to Student B, completing each sentence with the correct option. Student B will tell you if your answers are correct.

1 In the summer, you can see the sun for 24 hours a day in some places in *England / Norway / Australia*.

2 The first person to climb Mount Everest was from *the U.S. / New Zealand / the UK*.

3 Every year *fewer than ten / about 100 / over 1,000* people are killed by sharks.

4 The strongest hurricane ever had wind speeds of *100 / 320 / 600* kilometers an hour.

5 Mount Fuji is a volcano in *China / South Korea / Japan*.

2 Listen to Student B read facts 1–5. The correct answers are in **bold**. Tell Student B if his/her answers are correct.

1 The largest ocean in the world is the *Atlantic* / **Pacific** / *Indian* Ocean.

2 Lightning strikes the world *once* / **five times** / *100 times* a second.

3 Tornadoes are most common **on flat dry land** / *in hot countries* / *near the sea*.

4 At noon in July and August, the temperature in Riyadh, Saudi Arabia is usually *36* / **43** / *50* °C.

5 The longest river in the world is the *Mississippi* / **Nile** / *Amazon*.

11C Student A

1 Read problems 1–6 to Student B. He/She will respond.

1 I got up late. I missed the bus.
2 I didn't take a map. I got lost.
3 My car ran out of gas. I had to walk.
4 I stayed up late last night. I was exhausted this morning.
5 I didn't have any lunch. I was starving this afternoon.
6 I parked in front of the station. I got a parking fine.

2 Listen to Student B's sentences. Use the third conditional to respond.

B *I was late for a meeting. My boss was furious.*
A *If you had arrived on time, your boss wouldn't have been furious.*

11D Student A

1 Student B is going to take a trip this summer. Answer his/her questions using the information in the box.

1 You think California is more interesting.
2 San Francisco is a beautiful city and a good place to stay.
3 Yosemite is a great park for hiking.
4 The cost of food is reasonable. Particularly Mexican food, which is delicious.
5 The weather is always good. September is a good month to go.

2 You want to visit Australia or New Zealand. Ask Student B for recommendations using prompts 1–5.

1 Ask for a recommendation. Australia or New Zealand?
2 Ask which city to stay in.
3 Ask about hiking. Are there any good places?
4 You don't have much money. What about food?
5 Best time to go in terms of weather?

7D Student B

1 You are a tourist who is lost. You want to visit the museum. Ask Student A for directions using prompts 1–5.

  1 Ask for help politely.
  2 Ask for directions to the museum.
  3 Ask if it was left or right at the traffic light.
  4 Repeat the route and ask for confirmation.
  5 Thank him/her politely.

2 Student A is a tourist who is lost. You know the town well. Respond to Student A's questions and give directions using the information in the box.

> **The train station.** 5–6 minutes away on foot. Follow this street until you get to the traffic circle. Take a right and go straight ahead, over a bridge. The station is on the left after the bridge.

12A Student A

1 Read the sentences to Student B. Does he/she agree or disagree? Check (✔) the box if he/she agrees.

	Student B
1 I love relaxing vacations.	☐
2 I don't enjoy camping.	☐
3 I don't like spending all day at the beach.	☐
4 I'd love to travel around the U.S.	☐
5 I can't wait to go on vacation!	☐
6 I've already planned my next vacation.	☐

2 Listen to Student B. Look at your responses below. Respond with *so* or *neither* to agree (✔), or *I* + verb to disagree (**X**).

	Your responses
1 I usually go on vacation in this country.	✔
2 I haven't been away this year.	✔
3 I can't go away for a whole month.	**X**
4 I'd love to stay on the coast.	**X**
5 I didn't like that hotel very much.	✔
6 I'm looking forward to getting away.	✔

12C Student A

1 Read the clues below about the building in the photo. Follow the instructions.

  • After each clue, wait for Student B to make deductions.
  • After three clues, Student B can guess the answer.
  • If Student B's guess is wrong, give him/her the extra clue.

The Taj Mahal

Clue 1: It's not in the U.S.
Clue 2: It was built in the 17th century, in memory of a princess.
Clue 3: Both the interior and the exterior are beautifully decorated.
Extra clue: It's in India.

2 Look at the picture and the list of buildings and follow the instructions.

  • Listen to Student B's clues. After each clue, make deductions about which building it is.
  • After you hear three clues, give your answer.
  • If you're wrong, you can hear one more clue. Guess again.

The Great Wall of China	The Statue of Liberty
The Taj Mahal	The Great Pyramid of Giza
Machu Picchu	Big Ben

7A Student B

1 Look at the pictures and listen to Student A's questions. Choose the correct answer a–c.

1

  a tennis
  b soccer
  c cricket

2

  a five
  b eight
  c ten

3

  a the television
  b the radio
  c the Internet

4

  a in the 15th century
  b in the 17th century
  c in the 19th century

5

  a an alpaca and a condor
  b a lion and a swan
  c an owl and a bear

2 Ask Student A the trivia questions using the passive in the correct tense. The correct answer is in **bold**.

1 When / the Eiffel Tower / build?
  a 1789
  b **1889**
  c 1989

2 What / recently / discover / on the planet Mars?
  a plants
  b life
  c **water**

3 In which city / Europe and Asia / connect / by a bridge?
  a **Istanbul**
  b Moscow
  c Athens

4 How many babies / born / in the world every minute?
  a around 20
  b **around 200**
  c around 2000

5 What can / see / from the International Space Station?
  a the Great Pyramids at Giza
  b the Pentagon
  c **the Great Wall of China**

7C Student B

1 Answer Student A's questions. Give more information about each answer.

2 Ask Student A questions 1–5 using the correct form of *can*, *could*, or *be able to*.

  1 When you were eight years old, _____ you watch any TV shows that you wanted?
  2 Which musical instrument would you like to _____ play?
  3 Would you like to _____ sing like an opera singer?
  4 _____ you watch TV shows on your smartphone?
  5 _____ you ever _____ see your favorite band in concert?

8A Student B

1 Look at the facts about James Rodríguez in the chart. Student A will check these facts with you. Correct Student A's facts if necessary.

2 Look at the chart. You think the facts about Fabiana Claudino are correct but you're not 100% sure. Use statements with tag questions to check the facts with Student A.

James Rodríguez	
Sport	Soccer
Plays for	Real Madrid
Nationality	Colombian
Born	July 12th, 1991, Cúcuta
Height	1.80 m.
Career highlight	Winning the Champions League in 2016
Favorite players	Cristiano Ronaldo, LeBron James

Fabiana Claudino	
Sport	Volleyball
Nationality	Brazilian
Born	January 24th, 1986
Home city	Rio de Janeiro
Height	1.90 m.
Career highlight	Winning gold in the 2016 Olympic Games
Favorite type of movie	Romantic comedies

8C Student B

1 Listen to Student A. Respond using a sentence part 1–5 in column 1 and an ending a–e from column 2.

1 You're right. I have to	a feed the animals in the zoo.
2 You have to	b go to bed early tonight.
3 No! You can't	c be there two hours before the flight.
4 You don't have to	d buy her some flowers.
5 Yes, I do. I have to	e get up early today. It's Saturday.

2 Read sentences 1–5 to Student A. Listen to his/her replies. Correct the responses if necessary.

1 You look like you're out of shape these days.
   Response: I know. I have to start going to the gym again.
2 Why don't you wear a suit to work?
   Response: We don't have to dress up in my office.
3 Am I allowed to take a photo?
   Response: No. You can't use your camera in the museum.
4 Is the flight to New York direct?
   Response: No, it's not. You have to change in Miami.
5 Should I drive you to the station?
   Response: Thanks, but you don't have to. I can walk.

9A Student B

1 Listen to Student A's questions. Choose the correct response a–f.

a It was really exciting!
b That's great! What's the weather like there?
c No, I haven't. What's it like?
d Should we go to the movies?
e No, thanks. I'm full.
f Yes, I do. I eat everything!

2 Ask Student A questions 1–6. Student A will respond. Does the response make sense?

1 What's Tina like?
2 Would you like something to drink?
3 We went to that new Italian restaurant last night.
4 What does Ian look like?
5 Do you like orange juice?
6 Do you want to go out tonight?

9C Student B

1 Listen to Student A. Complete each sentence part with an ending a–f. Decide together if the completed sentences make sense.

a ... to be on time for the meeting.
b ... to make new friends when she goes to college.
c ... to go to the beach this summer.
d ... being late for his interview.
e ... making new friends.
f ... going abroad on vacation.

2 Read sentence parts 1–6 to Student A. He/She will complete them. Decide together if the completed sentences make sense.

1 On Saturday, I'd really like ...
2 Nicholas suggested ...
3 I'm thinking about ...
4 We can't afford to ...
5 Maria's looking forward to ...
6 Maria wants ...

9D Student B

1 You and Student A are going to order some takeout. Look at the menu and follow the instructions.

  1 Listen to Student A's suggestions.

  2 Respond negatively. Suggest two alternative dishes.

  3 Listen to Student A. Change your mind if you want, or agree to disagree. Choose a third dish if necessary.

MIMI's *takeout menu*

Vegetable lasagna	$10.25
Spicy chicken in coconut milk	$11.50
Lamb, mushroom, and spinach stew	$14
Oven-baked zucchini, eggplant, and potato	$10
Spicy beef burger, salad, and French fries	$12.50
Thai green curry with eggplant and mixed peppers	$9

10A Student B

1 Look at the story. Take turns with Student A and report what the people said. Listen to Student A and complete the missing dialogue.

2 Check your story with Student A. Do you have the same dialogue?

10C Student B

1 Listen and answer Student A's questions. Explain your decisions.

2 Ask Student A questions 1–4.

  1 If you saw a colleague stealing paper at work, would you …
    a say nothing?
    b tell your colleague to put it back?
    c tell your boss?

  2 If a friend gave you a horrible sweater for your birthday, would you …
    a say you already have one just like it, and exchange it for something else?
    b say thanks, smile, but never wear it?
    c say you don't like it?

  3 If a stranger asked to borrow your cell phone, would you …
    a say, "Sorry, I don't have one"?
    b say, "Sorry, I'm in a hurry"?
    c lend it to him/her?

  4 If your friend left her Facebook page open on your computer, would you …
    a close it because it's private?
    b update her status with something funny?
    c read her private messages?

11A Student B

1 Listen to Student A read facts 1–5. The correct answers are in **bold**. Tell Student A if his/her answers are correct.

 1 In the summer, you can see the sun for 24 hours a day in some places in *England* / **Norway** / *Australia*.
 2 The first person to climb Mount Everest was from *the U.S.* / **New Zealand** / *the UK*.
 3 Every year **fewer than ten** / *about 100* / *over 1,000* people are killed by sharks.
 4 The strongest hurricane ever had wind speeds of *100* / **320** / *600* kilometers an hour.
 5 Mount Fuji is a volcano in *China* / *South Korea* / **Japan**.

2 Read facts 1–5 to Student A, completing each sentence with the correct option. Student A will tell you if your answers are correct.

 1 The largest ocean in the world is the *Atlantic* / *Pacific* / *Indian* Ocean.
 2 Lightning strikes the world *once* / *five times* / *100 times* a second.
 3 Tornadoes are most common *on flat dry land* / *in hot countries* / *near the sea*.
 4 At noon in July and August, the temperature in Riyadh, Saudi Arabia is usually *36* / *43* / *50* °C.
 5 The longest river in the world is the *Mississippi* / *Nile* / *Amazon*.

11C Student B

1 Listen to Student A's sentences. Use the third conditional to respond.

 A *I got up late. I missed the bus.*
 B *If you hadn't gotten up late, you wouldn't have missed the bus.*

2 Read problems 1–6 to Student A. He/She will respond.

 1 I was late for a meeting. My boss was furious.
 2 I didn't take the garbage out. It smelled bad this morning.
 3 I didn't take an umbrella. I got wet.
 4 I forgot to text Dan. He didn't know about the party.
 5 I didn't lock my bike. It was stolen.
 6 I turned off my freezer. There was a flood in my kitchen.

11D Student B

1 You want to visit California or Florida. Ask Student A for recommendations using prompts 1–5.

 1 Ask for a recommendation. California or Florida?
 2 Ask which city to stay in.
 3 Ask about hiking. Are there any good places?
 4 You don't have much money. What about food?
 5 Best time to go in terms of weather?

2 Student A is going to visit Australia or New Zealand. Answer his/her questions using the information in the box.

 1 You think New Zealand is more interesting.
 2 Christchurch is a beautiful city and a good place to stay.
 3 South Island is a great place for hiking.
 4 The cost of food is reasonable. Particularly the pies.
 5 The weather can be wet. January is a good month to go.

12A Student B

1 Listen to Student A. Look at your responses below. Respond with *so* or *neither* to agree (✔), or *I* + verb to disagree (✗).

Your responses

 1 I love relaxing vacations. ✔
 2 I don't enjoy camping. ✔
 3 I don't like spending all day at the beach. ✗
 4 I'd love to travel around the U.S. ✔
 5 I can't wait to go on vacation! ✔
 6 I've already planned my next vacation. ✗

2 Read the sentences to Student A. Does he/she agree or disagree? Check (✔) the box if he/she agrees.

Student A

 1 I usually go on vacation in this country. ☐
 2 I haven't been on vacation this year. ☐
 3 I can't go away for a whole month. ☐
 4 I'd love to stay on the coast. ☐
 5 I didn't like that hotel very much. ☐
 6 I'm looking forward to getting away. ☐

12C Student B

1 Look at the picture and the list of buildings and follow the instructions.

- Listen to Student A's clues. After each clue, make deductions about which building it is.
- After you hear three clues, give your answer.
- If you're wrong, you can hear one more clue. Guess again.

The Great Wall of China	The Statue of Liberty
The Taj Mahal	The Great Pyramid of Giza
Machu Picchu	Big Ben

2 Read the clues below about the building in the photo. Follow the instructions.

- After each clue, wait for Student A to make deductions.
- After three clues, Student A can guess the answer.
- If Student A's guess is wrong, give him/her the extra clue.

Machu Picchu

Clue 1: It's not in Europe.
Clue 2: It was built in the 15th century and is made of stone.
Clue 3: Its name means "old peak."
Extra clue: It's in Peru.

Infinitive	Simple past	Past participle	Infinitive	Simple past	Past participle
be	was, were	been	lend	lent	lent
beat	beat	beaten	let	let	let
become	became	become	lie	lay	lain
begin	began	begun	lose	lost	lost
bite	bit	bitten	make	made	made
break	broke	broken	mean	meant	meant
bring	brought	brought	meet	met	met
build	built	built	pay	paid	paid
buy	bought	bought	put	put	put
catch	caught	caught	read /riːd/	read /red/	read /red/
choose	chose	chosen	ride	rode	ridden
come	came	come	ring	rang	rung
cost	cost	cost	rise	rose	risen
do	did	done	run	ran	run
draw	drew	drawn	say	said	said
drink	drank	drunk	see	saw	seen
drive	drove	driven	sell	sold	sold
eat	ate	eaten	send	sent	sent
fall	fell	fallen	shut	shut	shut
feel	felt	felt	sing	sang	sung
find	found	found	sit	sat	sat
fly	flew	flown	sleep	slept	slept
forbid	forbade	forbidden	speak	spoke	spoken
forget	forgot	forgotten	spend	spent	spent
forgive	forgave	forgiven	stand	stood	stood
get	got	gotten	steal	stole	stolen
give	gave	given	stick	stuck	stuck
go	went	gone, been	swim	swam	swum
grow	grew	grown	take	took	taken
have	had	had	teach	taught	taught
hear	heard	heard	tell	told	told
hide	hid	hidden	think	thought	thought
hit	hit	hit	throw	threw	thrown
hold	held	held	understand	understood	understood
hurt	hurt	hurt	wake	woke	woken
keep	kept	kept	wear	wore	worn
know	knew	known	win	won	won
leave	left	left	write	wrote	written

Personal
Best

Workbook

B1+
Intermediate

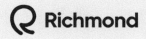
Richmond

Entertainment

7A — **LANGUAGE**

GRAMMAR: The passive

1 Choose the correct options to complete the sentences.

1 I don't have a computer at the moment. It _____.
   a is fixing   b is being fixed
   c fixes

2 Last year, he _____ in a traffic accident.
   a was injured   b injured
   c was being injured

3 Unwanted items can _____ to us at the above address.
   a be returning   b be returned
   c return

4 Sadly, much of the forest has now _____.
   a destroy   b destroyed
   c been destroyed

5 They just announced that the flight _____ by two hours.
   a is delaying   b will be delayed
   c will delay

6 The kitchen _____ at the moment.
   a is painted   b painting
   c is being painted

7 So much progress _____ in so little time.
   a been achieved   b has achieved
   c has been achieved

8 How much of your food _____ each week?
   a throws away   b is throwing away
   c is thrown away

2 Complete the sentences using the verbs in the box in the passive form with the prompts in parentheses.

> film   ring   invent   punish
> announce   advise   decorate

1 We can't go in the living room because it _____. (present continuous)

2 The electric battery _____ by Alessandro Volta. (simple past)

3 Those bells _____ at eleven o'clock every morning. (simple present)

4 She _____ by her doctor to stop taking the pills. (present perfect)

5 The results of the competition _____ as I arrived. (past continuous)

6 Some early scenes in the movie _____ in the studio. (future with *will*)

7 People _____ for their crimes. (+ *must*)

VOCABULARY: Movies

3 Order the letters to make movie words.

Zara So what movie did you see last night?
Raf   It was a Spanish movie, [1] **tse** _____ in Madrid. It's a [2] **leesqu** _____ to a movie that I saw last year.
Zara I didn't know you spoke Spanish!
Raf   I don't. But it had [3] **ibustlest** _____.
Zara I prefer it when foreign films are [4] **budbed** _____. Anyway, was it good?
Raf   The [5] **satc** _____ was fantastic, especially the main actor. It had a pretty complicated [6] **tolp** _____ that was sometimes hard to follow. What have you seen recently?
Zara I saw a [7] **rorohr** _____ movie last week.
Raf   Oh no, I can't stand blood!
Zara I know, but it was good, and really funny at times.
Raf   Who wrote the [8] **tcrisp** _____ for it?
Zara I don't know, but the main character was [9] **depaly** _____ by Douglas Booth. And the [10] **nostudrack** _____ was amazing. I've been listening to it on my headphones all morning.

4 Complete the movie words.

1 Ian likes ac_____ _____ _____ _____ movies with lots of fights.

2 The movie will be re_____ _____ _____ _____ _____ _____ next spring.

3 The movie's special ef_____ _____ _____ _____ _____ were amazing, especially the ones in space.

4 We watched a do_____ _____ _____ _____ _____ _____ about the final years of the artist's life.

5 The wedding sc_____ _____ _____ at the end was hilarious.

6 My favorite movies are ba_____ _____ _____ on real-life stories.

7 It was a science-fi_____ _____ _____ _____ movie, set in the 25th century.

8 Sarah knows all the songs from that mu_____ _____ _____ _____ _____.

PRONUNCIATION: Past participles

5 ▶ 7.1 Match the vowels in the underlined words with a–d. Say the sentences aloud. Then listen, check, and repeat.

a /ow/   b /ɑ/   c /ʌ/   d /ɔ/

1 Both movies had been underlined into Italian. _____

2 The movie was watched by 9.2 million viewers. _____

3 Which actor was chosen to play the part? _____

4 Her lines were spoken by a different person. _____

5 The movie won three Oscars. _____

6 The plot is about a lost astronaut. _____

READING: Guessing the meaning of words from context

The best method?

While Daniel Day-Lewis was playing the lead role in the movie *Lincoln*, he is reported to have started signing his text messages "A" for Abraham, so entangled had his identity become with his screen character. His friends found [a]this strange, but it was all part of the way he worked.

Day-Lewis was practicing "method acting," a technique developed by the Russian actor and director Konstantin Stanislavski. Ideas about method acting have evolved over the years, but the central aim has always been for the actor to achieve complete emotional identification with the character he or she is playing. In practice, [b]that often means preparing for a role by having the same experiences as the character or, at the very least, making an effort to learn as much as possible about such experiences.

Such preparations can take many forms. Actors may move to another country and immerse themselves in an unfamiliar culture. They might learn a language or a skill such as horseriding or playing a musical instrument, or interview people who witnessed a particular event. Some actors, however, take things further. Much, much further. Christian Bale, for example, shed a massive 28 kilos to play Trevor Reznik, a man with severe psychological problems, in *The Machinist*, while Jamie Foxx actually glued his eyes together to bring added authenticity to his role as the blind musician Ray Charles. However, it was so uncomfortable that he soon gave [c]this up.

Probably the most famous recent example of extreme method acting is Leonardo DiCaprio in *The Revenant*. DiCaprio put himself through an unbelievably punishing regime of sleeping out in the wilderness, swimming in freezing rivers, and even eating the raw flesh of a bison (and he's a vegetarian!). [d]That gave him a real taste of the life he was about to portray.

Sadly for him, however, not everyone appreciated his efforts, with some people seeing them primarily as an attempt to gain the Oscar that had been eluding him for so long. [e]This meant that the Internet was soon awash with spoof posters showing DiCaprio's character in various desperate situations, with captions such as: "Do this man a favor. Just give him his Oscar!"

1 Read the article and choose the best options to complete the sentences.

1 Daniel Day-Lewis wrote "A" on his texts because
   a he admired Abraham Lincoln so much.
   b he confused himself with Abraham Lincoln.
   c he didn't want people to know who they were from.

2 In method acting, the actor aims to
   a look as much like the character as possible.
   b use a range of different acting methods.
   c think the same way as the character.

3 If a movie is about a particular event in history, the actor can find out more by
   a reading interviews with people who were there.
   b learning more about history.
   c talking to people who were there.

4 Leonardo DiCaprio suffered a lot because
   a his director wanted the scenes to look realistic.
   b he wanted to have a better understanding of his character.
   c he thought it would make people see the movie.

5 Some people joked about DiCaprio's method acting because
   a they thought that his acting still wasn't good enough to win an Oscar.
   b they didn't believe that what he did was very difficult.
   c they thought he was making it obvious that he wanted an Oscar.

2 Find the words in bold in the text. Look at the immediate context and choose the best options.

1 If two things are **entangled**, they are *joined together / damaging one another / difficult to understand*.

2 If something **evolves**, it *changes completely / changes suddenly / changes gradually*.

3 If you **immerse** yourself in something, you *spend a lot of time doing or experiencing it / try to copy it / strongly dislike it*.

4 **Authenticity** means being *impressive / real / painful*.

5 If something **eludes** you, you *want it very much / almost achieve it / do not manage to achieve it*.

6 A **spoof** is a *humorous version / a criticism / an illegal version* of something.

3 Match a–e (*this* and *that*) in the text with meanings 1–8. There are three extra meanings.

1 the fact that method acting has changed _____
2 writing "A" on his text messages _____
3 learning to ride a horse or play an instrument _____
4 sticking his eyes together _____
5 trying to understand a character's emotions very thoroughly _____
6 people thinking he wanted an Oscar _____
7 the fact that he has never won an Oscar _____
8 doing physically difficult things _____

GRAMMAR: Modals of ability and possibility

1 Order the words to make sentences.

1 to / paint / to / she'd / able / like / be

_____

2 able / never / to / swim / he's / been

_____

3 be / later / call / I'll / you / to / able

_____

4 meet / are / to / tonight / able / us / you

_____?

5 they / see / movie / able / the / weren't / to

_____

6 being / ride / he / to / motorcycle / able / a / loves

_____

7 we / the / museum / to / be / visit / won't / able

_____

8 to / a / haven't / able / I / buy / ticket / been

_____

2 Read the sentences and complete the replies with the correct form of *can* or *be able to*. There may be more than one answer.

1 A Are you coming to the concert next Saturday?
  B No, I'm afraid we're both working, so we _____.

2 A The best thing about vacations is all the books you can read!
  B Yes, I love _____ read all day. It's so relaxing.

3 A Why is she taking a math course?
  B She wants _____ help her son when he's older.

4 A I didn't know you were injured, Jamie.
  B It's pretty bad. I _____ play any sports since January.

5 A Did you ask Ethan about the trip?
  B No, he was in a meeting all day yesterday, so I _____ contact him.

6 A I'll bring the groceries back on my bike.
  B Will you _____ manage OK?

7 A I heard that Suzi is sick.
  B Yes, she _____ get out of bed for three days.

8 A I get so upset when I can't sleep.
  B Me, too! I really hate _____ sleep.

VOCABULARY: TV and music

3 Replace the underlined words with the nouns in the box.

album   band   track   playlist
channel   episode   host   audience

1 The person who introduces the show got into trouble after being rude to his guest.   _____

2 I switched to another TV station to watch a music show.   _____

3 I've just downloaded their latest collection of songs.   _____

4 Someone from the people watching the show asked him a question.   _____

5 I've been watching a series about a boy band; tonight it's the last part of the story.   _____

6 What's on your choice of music for the party?   _____

7 Which is your favorite group of musicians?   _____

8 The second song on the CD is probably the best.   _____

4 Complete the sentences with TV and music words.

1 I watched the first episode in the _____, but there are four more parts to go.

2 They had a few successful records, but *Get by* was probably their biggest _____.

3 The next time my favorite singer goes _____ _____, I'm definitely buying a ticket!

4 I have all her music, but I've never seen her perform _____ on stage.

5 He entered a TV _____ _____ and won first prize for singing.

6 There's a new _____ _____ on Channel 4 tonight about people marrying total strangers!

7 My mom loves this _____ _____ about a typical small town. It's been on TV for over twenty years.

8 I can't stand all the _____ they show between TV episode.

PRONUNCIATION: /eɪ/ and /ʊ/ sounds

5 ▶ 7.2   Practice saying the sentences. Make sure that you pronounce the vowel sound in *able* /eɪ/ and the vowel sound in *could* /ʊ/. Listen, check, and repeat.

1 I'd love to be able to play the guitar.

2 The music was so loud I couldn't hear Diego.

3 I won't be able to join you this year.

4 Luckily, I was able to take some time off.

5 She could play three instruments by the time she was ten.

6 We couldn't contact her yesterday.

SPEAKING: Giving directions

1 ▶7.3 Frida wants to go to a shoe store. Listen to the two conversations and complete the directions.

First store

1 It's _____ Grover Street.

2 From here, keep _____ _____ until you get to the _____.

3 When you get to the museum, _____ _____.

4 Go _____ the hill and _____ the movie theater on your _____.

5 Royal's is just a little bit farther, on the _____ _____ of the street.

Second store

6 _____ this street to the end.

7 Take a _____ _____ Cooper Street.

8 After that, you need to _____ the _____ _____.

9 It's _____ _____ a pizzeria.

2 Number these sentences 1–8 to make a conversation.

a Yes, it's across from the bus station. _____

b Yes, I did. It's next to a shopping center. _____

c That's right – you've got it! _____

d Of course. Take the first right at the traffic light, then go straight ahead. It's on the right. _____

e Excuse me, do you know where the library is? _____

f Sorry, did you say across from the bus station? _____

g And can you tell me how to get there, please? _____

h So, it's the first right, then straight ahead, and it's on the right? _____

3 Order the words to make indirect questions.

1 tell / you / bank / me / could / is / where / the
_____ ?

2 bus station / where / you / do / the / is / know
_____ ?

3 if / know / is / drugstore / near / you / there / a / here / do
_____ ?

4 name / you / is / the / this / could / tell / what / me / street / of
_____ ?

5 which / you / museum / could / is / on / tell / street / me / the
_____ ?

6 bus / this / stadium / know / do / the / stops / you / if / near
_____ ?

4 ▶7.4 Complete the conversation. Then listen and check.

A Sorry to ¹_____ you, but ²_____ you tell me where the hospital is?

B Yes, it's about ten minutes ³_____ car from here. You need to drive up Castle Hill, and ⁴_____ right when you get to the traffic light.

A So, it's ⁵_____ the hill and then make a ⁶_____?

B That's right. Then ⁷_____ the first left after the big traffic circle. Go ⁸_____ ahead ⁹_____ you see the hospital ¹⁰_____ the left.

A And do you ¹¹_____ if I can park there?

B Yes, just ¹²_____ the road around and you'll find the parking lot next to the main hospital building.

5 Think of two places in a town or city you know. Write an explanation of how to get from one to the other.

HOME   BLOG   **PODCASTS**   ABOUT   CONTACT

Tom and Sam talk about movies and TV.

LISTENING

1 ▶ **7.5** Listen to the podcast. Check (✓) the statement which is NOT true.

1   Sam prefers watching television to going to the movies.   _____

2   Rosie likes television series more than movies.   _____

3   Tom has more or less the same opinion as the caller, Rosie.   _____

2 ▶ **7.5** Listen again. Are the sentences true (T), false (F) or doesn't say (DS)?

1   In Sam's opinion, it is better to see a movie at the theater.   _____

2   Tom and Sam often go to the movies together.   _____

3   Rosie thinks that Hollywood likes making original movies.   _____

4   In Rosie's opinion, movie companies do not use new writers very often.   _____

5   Rosie's favorite directors never make TV series.   _____

6   In TV series, there is not enough time to develop the characters.   _____

7   Rosie thinks that the best actors always want to act in Hollywood movies.   _____

READING

1 Read Kate's blog on page 47 and choose the best summary of what a movie extra does, according to Kate.

a   They never speak and spend most of their time waiting.

b   They almost never speak and spend most of their time waiting.

c   They never speak, and they sometimes do not even appear in the movie.

2 Choose the correct options to complete the sentences.

1   According to Kate, extras
   a   are never recognized by their friends.
   b   usually take part in long science-fiction movies.
   c   usually appear only for a few seconds, often in groups.

2   Kate's mother did not see her daughter in the movie because
   a   she fell asleep at one point.
   b   Kate did not appear in it.
   c   she was too busy to go to the movies.

3   For most of the time, extras
   a   read books.
   b   listen to the director.
   c   do very little.

4   Most scenes in Kate's latest movie take place in
   a   London.
   b   a town outside of New York.
   c   elsewhere in the UK.

5   Kate didn't see any famous actors because
   a   it was too cold.
   b   they weren't in her part of the movie.
   c   they were all in the UK.

6   At the end of her blog, Kate sounds
   a   amused.
   b   disappointed.
   c   embarrassed.

HOME   **BLOG**   PODCASTS   ABOUT   CONTACT

Guest blogger Kate writes about working as a movie extra.

EXTRA SPECIAL

Here's something you may not know about me. Every now and then, I work as an extra on movie sets. Yes, I'm one of those people that you might just see in a crowd when you're watching a movie. Or not … If you don't pay close attention, you'll miss me! In fact, even if you are able to keep your eyes open for the entire movie, you still might not see me. Two years ago, my poor mother sat through one of those incredibly long science-fiction movies, which, as we all know, is her least favorite type of movie, because she wanted to see her daughter being killed by a robot. Sadly, unknown to her (and me), by the time the movie was released, that particular scene had been cut, and my mother had wasted three hours of her busy life.

People often ask me what it's like to work as an extra on a movie set. Well, extras are sometimes referred to as "moving furniture," and this seems about right to me. We don't speak (or rather we rarely speak, although, of course, if we do, we're paid more). We're simply there to provide the background for the main action. Most of our time is spent hanging around, just waiting for the director to tell us when we're needed. Often, we sit around in a trailer waiting for the call, though, and depending on the movie, we may also spend a large part of our day putting on costumes and being made up by the make-up artists. It's a job that requires patience – and a fully charged smartphone! (Oh my goodness, what did extras do before smartphones? A book is fine for a trailer, but you can't hide it in your costume when you're in the middle of a scene!) Obviously, I can't give you any of the details about my most recent job (top secret until it's released). I will just say that, although the majority of the movie is set in London, one scene was shot in a small town not far from New York. And that's where I came in. On a freezing cold winter day, dressed in just a light dress, with bare legs. (In the movie, it was late spring!) The main characters in the cast were played by really well-known British stars, but although some of them were in the U.S., none of them featured in my scene, unfortunately. So, no, I didn't meet any famous actors this time. Oh, and in case you're wondering, it wasn't the new Bond movie that's being released next month. Not this time …

Sports and health

8A | **LANGUAGE**

GRAMMAR: Tag questions

1 Choose the correct tag questions to complete the sentences.

1 She's really nice, *isn't it / isn't she / is she*?
2 You don't have Jamie's cell phone, *don't you / have you / do you*?
3 They were at the festival, *weren't they / didn't they / were they*?
4 Millie just got a new job, *doesn't she / didn't she / hasn't she*?
5 We're seeing you on Saturday, *aren't we / won't we / are we*?
6 Dan and Lucy are leaving, *aren't they / won't they / are they*?
7 It won't cause any problems, *won't it / does it / will it*?
8 Isabel speaks Spanish, *doesn't Isabel / doesn't she / does she*?
9 We should take a gift, *should we / shouldn't we / won't we*?
10 I can't call you at work, *will I / can I / can't I*?

2 Look at the tag questions. Then complete the sentences with the verbs in parentheses.

1 Ben _____ (go) to a gym in town, doesn't he?
2 Taylor _____ (come) in first in the race, didn't she?
3 They _____ (invite) Joe, have they?
4 You _____ (play) hockey, do you?
5 It _____ (be) an exciting game, won't it?
6 You _____ (bring) your phone, haven't you?
7 Tom _____ (be) at the game last night, was he?
8 We _____ (be) late, will we?
9 Antonio _____ (drive) us there, couldn't he?
10 They _____ (have to) pay for the service, should they?
11 You _____ (take) care of it, won't you?
12 He _____ (tell) Alia, did he?

VOCABULARY: Sports, places and equipment

3 Complete the sentences with the words in the box.

| pool | ice skating | circuit | net | track and field | goal | bat | field |

1 She runs and jumps well, so she's really good at _____.
2 Halfway through the soccer game, he left the _____.
3 That's the _____ where Rachel swims each morning.
4 She kicked the ball well, but just missed the _____.
5 He hit the ball hard with his _____.
6 I love watching the cars race around the _____.
7 She jumped high and tried to hit the ball over the _____.
8 In winter, they go _____ on the frozen lake.

4 Read the definitions and complete the words.

1 This object is used for hitting a ball. It has a long handle and a round part.   r__ __ __ __ __
2 This large, flat area is often covered with ice and is used for skating on.   r__ __ __
3 You play this game with a brown ball that is the shape of an egg.   f__ __ __ __ __ __ __
4 You wear these to protect your eyes in the water.   g__ __ __ __ __ __
5 In this event, fast cars go around a road in the shape of a ring.   a__ __ __ r__ __ __ __
6 An area for playing games like tennis, marked with lines.   c__ __ __ __
7 In this sport, you enter the water, usually with your head first.   d__ __ __ __ __
8 In this sport, you hit a small hard ball with a bat.   b__ __ __ __ __ __ __
9 This ring-shaped path is used for running around.   t__ __ __ __

PRONUNCIATION: Intonation

5 ▶ 8.1 Listen to the sentences. Match them with a or b.

a asking a real question (intonation goes up)
b making a comment (intonation goes down)

1 They play tennis, don't they? _____
2 Alfonso doesn't eat meat, does he? _____
3 Laura wasn't at Amanda's house, was she? _____
4 You don't like swimming, do you? _____
5 John and Adrian aren't coming, are they? _____
6 You'll get there in time, won't you? _____

LISTENING: Understanding facts and figures

1 ▶ 8.2 Daisy is asking her friend Luke about marathon running. Read the questions and circle the type of information you need to listen for. Then listen and answer the questions.

1 How long is a marathon in kilometers?
date / length of time / distance / price / number
Answer _____

2 How many marathons has Luke run?
date / length of time / distance / price / number
Answer _____

3 When did Luke run his first marathon?
date / length of time / distance / price / number
Answer _____

4 How long did his first marathon take?
date / length of time / distance / price / number
Answer _____

5 How long does it take Luke to run a marathon now?
date / length of time / distance / price / number
Answer _____

6 When is the Asheville, North Carolina Marathon?
date / length of time / distance / price / number
Answer _____

7 How long is it until the Asheville Marathon?
date / length of time / distance / price / number
Answer _____

8 When training for a marathon, by how much should you increase your distance each week?
date / length of time / distance / price / number
Answer _____

9 How much does the Boston Marathon cost runners?
date / length of time / distance / price / number
Answer _____

10 How many steps does the Great Wall Marathon have?
date / length of time / distance / price / number
Answer _____

2 ▶ 8.3 Underline the part or parts of the sentences where you expect the intonation to fall. Listen, check, and repeat.

1 Make sure you have days off so your muscles can recover.

2 The first marathon ever was in Athens.

3 Joe gets up at five every morning to have time to run.

4 I stopped training because I injured my leg.

5 Laura uses a pedometer to count her steps.

6 Swimming practice starts at eight this morning.

7 I run faster if I run with friends.

8 Take plenty of water in case you get thirsty.

3 Complete the words.

1 Jenny has been trying to eat more, but she is still u __ __ __ __ __ __ __ __ __.

2 Many illnesses are caused by people having an unhealthy l __ __ __ __ __ __ __ __.

3 Peter's on a d __ __ __ at the moment because he wants to lose weight for his wedding.

4 Make sure you eat a b __ __ __ __ __ __ diet with plenty of vegetables and fish.

5 I usually eat healthy food, but I have a few bad h __ __ __ __ __ like buying potato chips on my way back from work.

6 Tia finds that regular exercise helps her to get a good night's s __ __ __ __.

7 It's a good idea to do some e __ __ __ __ __ __ __ before you go on a skiing vacation.

8 Laurence is o __ __ __ __ __ __ __ __ because he eats a lot of cheese.

9 Tanya really got in s __ __ __ __ when she worked as a tennis coach.

10 It's easy to get s __ __ __ __ __ __ __ out if you don't have enough time to prepare for an important competition.

GRAMMAR: Modals of obligation and advice

1 Choose the correct options to complete the sentences.

1 You _____ come to my parents' house with me. I can go on my own.
   a can't   b shouldn't   c don't have to

2 If you're not there, they'll leave without you, so you _____ be late.
   a can't   b don't have to   c must

3 I'm a bit tired today. I _____ work eleven hours yesterday.
   a have to   b had to   c can

4 You _____ look at screens before bedtime as it stops you from sleeping.
   a have to   b don't have to   c shouldn't

5 I'm wondering what to do. Perhaps I _____ speak to Sarah.
   a can't   b have to   c should

6 If Lara is away next week, she will _____ cancel her doctor's appointment.
   a have to   b can   c should

7 I _____ remember Magda's birthday this year. Isn't she turning 40?
   a can't   b should   c have to

8 Do we _____ finish the report by Friday? There is still so much to do.
   a had to   b have to   c allowed to

2 Complete 1–6 with *should* or the correct form of *have to*. There may be more than one answer.

Raj	How are you doing with the packing? Have you asked Luke to bring some cooking equipment?
Naomi	No, not yet. He's still on the plane. I'll ¹_____ speak to him later when he lands.
Raj	I hear it's going to be freezing cold this weekend, so we ²_____ take the extra-warm sleeping bags.
Naomi	They're already in the car! By the way, be ready for an early start tomorrow morning! I know you hate ³_____ get up early, but we're leaving at six.
Raj	Oh, really? Do we ⁴_____ leave so early?
Naomi	Don't you remember last year? We ⁵_____ sit in traffic for two hours because it was so busy.
Raj	You're right. I'd forgotten about that. I really ⁶_____ get to bed early!

3 Complete the conversations with the correct form of *have to*, *can*, or *should*.

1 A Dan doesn't know about the problem yet.
   B He doesn't? Perhaps you _____ tell him at all.

2 A Would you like us to bring any food this evening?
   B Well, we'll have plenty, so you _____.

3 A We just missed the bus!
   B Oh, well. We'll just _____ get the next one.

4 A So does Sam know about the party?
   B Absolutely not! It's a surprise for his birthday, so you _____ tell him!

5 A See you at the airport at nine o'clock.
   B Great! And remember, this time you _____ bring your passport!

6 A Charlie always looks lonely. He doesn't seem to have many friends.
   B I think we _____ ask him to go to the movies with us?

7 A I don't feel so good. I think I'm getting a cold.
   B Well, perhaps you _____ go out tonight.

8 A Why were you at the meeting?
   B My boss wasn't able to attend, so I _____ go.

9 A There's a managers' meeting in Toronto next month, and I'd like Julia to attend.
   B Does she _____ go? She's very busy right now.

10 A Marco loves his summer job. He's working nights at a restaurant on the beach.
   B Sounds perfect for him. He _____ get up early!

PRONUNCIATION: Sentence stress

4 ▶ 8.4 Read the sentences and <u>underline</u> the verbs of obligation and advice you think will be stressed. Listen, check, and repeat.

1 You have to call your brother.
2 He should speak to James first.
3 You shouldn't work so hard.
4 I have to remember to take my phone.
5 She can't tell Alfonso.
6 You don't have to reserve.
7 Adam will have to call her and explain.
8 I guess I should complain.

WRITING: Writing a report

HOW TO BE AN ACTIVE ADULT

(1) Most adults stay in shape / Most adults don't get enough exercise
It is recommended that all adults should do at least 150 minutes of moderate aerobic activity a week. However, 30% of adults exercise for less than 30 minutes per week.

(2) The benefits of exercise / Too much exercise can be bad for you
It is well known that physical activity has a number of positive results. It reduces the risk of many illnesses such as heart disease and even cancer. Moreover, exercise improves our mental health and can help us to lose weight.

(3) Practice a sport every day / Exercise a little every day
We all lead very busy lives, so it can be difficult to find enough time for exercise. I suggest having shorter periods of activity – perhaps ten minutes here and there throughout the day. In addition, you should try to incorporate exercise into your everyday activities. For example, you can walk up and down while you are on the phone, or why not use the stairs instead of taking the elevator?

(4) Spend less time working / Turn off your screens
Many of us spend far too much time sitting down, often in front of a screen. It is easy to spend the evening watching TV after a long day at work.In addition to this, spending time online can take up a lot of our day. All of this is time when we are hardly moving our bodies, so you should try to switch off and do something more active instead.

(5) Be active together / Get more exercise
Most things are more fun if you do them with someone else, and exercise is no exception. If you plan to go swimming with a friend, you are less likely to change your mind and stay at home. I would also recommend finding a physical activity that the whole family can enjoy – that way you can get in shape and spend quality time together, as well.

1 Read the report about exercise. Choose the best heading for each paragraph (1–5).

2 Complete the sentences with the words and phrases in the box and add commas where necessary. There may be more than one answer.

> as well   as well as   in addition to this
> in addition   moreover

1 It can be difficult for some children to find time for sports _____ their homework and other activities.
2 Too much time on a computer can make children get out of shape. _____ it can lead to sleep problems.
3 Children who love swimming may enjoy other water sports _____.
4 Bicycling is a great way for children to get in shape. _____ it is a great activity for families to do together.
5 Many schools arrange after-school sports clubs. _____ you can often find local clubs that organize activities in the evenings or on the weekend.

3 Think of ways to encourage children to be more active. Complete the sentences with your ideas.

1 To make sports more fun for your child, I would recommend doing some activities together.
2 When you take your children swimming, remember to _____.
3 If your child hates team sports, I suggest _____.
4 If your child does not play many sports at school, I recommend _____.
5 If your children do a lot of hard physical activity, remember to _____.
6 To encourage your child to watch less TV, I suggest _____.

4 Write a report about encouraging children to be more active. Use ideas from exercises 2 and 3, as well as your own ideas.

- Plan four or five section headings.
- Include factual information.
- Make recommendations using *suggest* or *recommend + -ing,* or *remember*.
- Use the words and phrases from exercise 2 to add information.

HOME   BLOG   PODCASTS   ABOUT   CONTACT

Learning Curve

Tom and Sam talk about National Get Outdoors Day.

LISTENING

1 ▶ 8.5 Listen to the podcast and number a–f in the order that you hear them (1–6).

a Hugo's reasons for taking part in National Get Outdoors Day _____

b the advantages of getting exercise outdoors _____

c how Hugo plans to lose weight this time _____

d Tom's plans for National Get Outdoors Day _____

e Hugo's plans for National Get Outdoors Day _____

f what Hugo eats when he gets stressed out _____

2 ▶ 8.5 Listen again and choose the correct options to complete the sentences.

1 The main aim of National Get Outdoors Day is to encourage people to
  a go outside and enjoy nature.
  b go outside and do some physical activity.
  c spend some time with their friends outdoors.

2 Hugo has planned to
  a play volleyball and soccer.
  b play soccer and have lunch outside.
  c play volleyball and soccer and have lunch outside.

3 Hugo tells Sam and Tom that he is
  a slightly overweight.
  b very overweight.
  c not at all overweight.

4 Hugo says he is hoping to lose weight by
  a playing more soccer.
  b being more active.
  c eating less.

5 What example of a bad habit does Sam give?
  a driving instead of walking
  b eating chocolate
  c bicycling instead of walking

6 Sam says being outdoors makes her
  a eat less.
  b exercise more.
  c feel less stressed out.

READING

1 Read Taylor's blog on page 49 and choose the best summary.

a It is very important for people to get plenty of exercise every day.

b Some of the advice about exercise on the Internet is very strange.

c We should not give other people advice about how to exercise.

2 Are the sentences true (T), false (F), or doesn't say (DS)?

1 Taylor doesn't exercise every day. _____

2 She thinks we should all spend more time exercising. _____

3 She says that it is hard for busy people to find enough time to exercise. _____

4 She thinks it is a good idea to wear the same clothes to exercise and sleep in. _____

5 She always wears pajamas in bed. _____

6 She thinks it is a bad idea to exercise while waiting in line. _____

7 She thinks conversation might be difficult during a "sports date." _____

8 She recommends wearing red clothes while you are exercising. _____

3 Find words or phrases from the text that mean:

1 someone who helps you exercise

2 a reminder of the things you need to do

3 night clothes

4 get exercise

5 can't breathe easily

6 water produced by the skin

HOME   **BLOG**   PODCASTS   ABOUT   CONTACT

Guest blogger Taylor writes about advice on exercise.

EXERCISE MAD

You all know that I work as a personal trainer and that I'm crazy about yoga, so you might expect me to recommend getting some serious exercise every day. But you'd be wrong. Exercise is great – I'm a big fan – but most of us have a lot more going on in our lives than going to the gym, don't we?

In an ideal world, we'd all have an hour a day in which to get in shape. However, in the real world, 24 hours is often not enough time to work (or go to school), spend time with our family, and get eight hours' sleep. Some days, exercise just comes lower down the to-do list. And that's totally fine.

But that's clearly not how everyone feels. Lately, I've been reading some really strange advice on the Internet, given by people who take fitness very seriously. Some of it is so weird I feel the need to share it with you:

• "*You should wear your exercise clothes to bed. Then, you can get up and go for that early-morning run right away.*" Sounds reasonable, doesn't it? No, it does not! The clothes that we exercise in are fitted and tight. And the clothes we sleep in are designed to be loose and cool and comfortable. You don't really want to sweat all night in your yoga pants, do you? Surely you'd rather get a good night's sleep in your pajamas, wouldn't you?

• "*While you're waiting in line, why not get a bit of exercise? Yes, folks, if you're standing in line at the supermarket checkout, and you have nothing to do, why not work out? If you're waiting at the airport for a delayed flight, why not get out your yoga mat?*" Because that will look really normal, won't it? And, what's more, if there's anyone within a couple of meters of you, with all that jumping around and waving of arms, it might even be dangerous!

• "*Make a sports date with your new girlfriend or boyfriend. A run or a session at the gym is a great way to get to know someone, isn't it?*" Especially when you're so out of breath that you can't even talk to the person! And, I'm sure you would agree, wouldn't you, that we all want to look our best when we go on a date – not red-faced and covered in sweat after half an hour at the gym!

• "*You should wear red when you exercise. This powerful color can give you extra energy while you try to get in shape.*" Honestly, who writes this stuff? They can't really believe it, can they?

UNIT 9 Food

9A LANGUAGE

GRAMMAR: Uses of *like*

1 Complete the conversation with the words and phrases in the box.

> feel like   was it like   seems like
> would like   like   doesn't like   is like
> would you like

A We went to the new Italian restaurant in town last night.

B Oh, you did? What ¹_____?

A Great. I loved it. I really ²_____ Italian food – it's my favorite, and this was one of the best. You and Chris should go there sometime.

B I really ³_____ to go, but you know what Chris ⁴_____! He ⁵_____ any kind of Mediterranean food. In fact, he doesn't really like eating out at all.

A Oh no! That's such a shame!

B Yes, sometimes I ⁶_____ leaving him at home and going out with friends, instead.

A Well that ⁷_____ a great idea to me! ⁸_____ to come with us the next time we go? We'd be very happy to have you join us!

2 Use the prompts to write sentences with the correct use of *like*.

1 Molly/like/swimming. She's afraid of water.

_____

2 I'm/teacher/but/like/be/writer.

_____

3 what/the concert/like/last night?

_____

4 you/like/go/movies/this evening?

_____

5 My grandmother's great! I/want/like/her.

_____

6 What is this meat? It/taste/like/chicken.

_____

VOCABULARY: Food and cooking

3 Order the letters to make food words.

1 I didn't feel like cooking last night, so we got **koteatu** _____ pizza for dinner.

2 Supermarket cakes are never as nice as **ehomedam** _____ ones.

3 We dipped pieces of bread in a big pot of **teldem** _____ cheese.

4 It was a simple meal – a piece of **lerdigl** _____ fish on rice.

5 Would you like some **tedrag** _____ cheese on your pasta?

6 I sometimes have a **lobied** _____ egg and toast for breakfast.

7 They sell bread and cakes and other **kabde** _____ products.

8 Serve the dish with **lisdec** _____ tomatoes on top.

4 Complete the sentences with food words.

1 S_____h are small sea creatures with hard coverings that you can eat.

2 O_____ o_____ is often used for salad dressings, sometimes with vinegar or lemon juice.

3 An a_____o has dark green skin, a large stone, and green flesh that is soft and not sweet.

4 A s_____ is a thick flat piece of meat, usually from a cow.

5 A_____s is a green vegetable with long, thin stems.

6 G_____ is white and grows under the ground. It has a very strong taste!

7 A z_____i is long and usually has dark green skin. It has seeds and contains a lot of water.

8 A L_____ is a small fruit like a lemon with green skin and sour juice.

PRONUNCIATION: /dʒ/

5 ▶ 9.1 Listen to the sentences. Are *do you* and *would you* pronounced with /dy/ or /dʒ/ sounds? Listen again and repeat.

1	What would you like to do now?	/dy/	/dʒ/
2	What do you like doing in the evenings?	/dy/	/dʒ/
3	Would you like to come with us?	/dy/	/dʒ/
4	Do you like dancing?	/dy/	/dʒ/
5	What would you like for lunch?	/dy/	/dʒ/
6	Where do you like to go on vacation?	/dy/	/dʒ/
7	When do you want to go?	/dy/	/dʒ/
8	Where do you want to meet?	/dy/	/dʒ/

READING: Reading for detail

Can you have a healthy diet on a low budget?
Yes, says Bonnie Naylor, if you follow these tips.

A   Eat before you shop
Going to the supermarket on an empty stomach is a recipe for over spending! You simply won't be able to resist that extra bar of chocolate or that yummy-looking piece of cheese. So eat first and go with a list – having [1]one and sticking to it is a great way to avoid waste.

B   Stay local
Remember, too, that if something is grown in a far-away country, you are paying for transportation as well as the food itself. Avocados may be cheap in Mexico, but in London, they're still a bit of a luxury. And why buy carrots from halfway around the world when [2]ones from your own country are cheaper and taste just the same?

C   A new best friend!
When you're on a tight budget, lentils are your best friend! Low in calories, packed with fiber, vitamins, and minerals – what's not to like? Look online for tasty lentil recipes – there are some great [3]ones around. Try other legumes, too – use chickpeas to replace half the chicken in a curry, for example. You'll save money, and it will taste just as good.

D   Go wild (well, a bit!)
I'm not suggesting you go out hunting a deer (although apparently "survival" vacations where participants have to kill and prepare any meat they eat are becoming increasingly popular with urban office workers). Foraging is the name of the game – in the woods for mushrooms, nuts, and berries,

or on the seashore for shellfish or even edible seaweed. A word of warning though – you need to educate yourself first! The right kind of mushroom is about the most delicious thing you can imagine; the wrong [4]one could kill you.

E   Beware the BOGOF!
Look out for special offers of course, but they need to be the right [5]ones. Don't be tempted by "Buy One Get One Free" offers unless they're for something you actually want – can you really eat two very ripe pineapples within 24 hours? A better bet is to go to the market near the end of the day.

1 Read the text quickly then <u>underline</u> the key words in the questions in exercise 2. Write A–E for the paragraph where you think you will find the answer.

1 _____   5 _____
2 _____   6 _____
3 _____   7 _____
4 _____

2 Read the text again and choose the correct options.

1 Why is it a bad idea to shop when you are hungry?
   a You will need to buy extra food to fill up.
   b You will want to buy things that you do not need.
   c You will do your shopping too quickly and make bad choices.

2 How can you avoid buying things you don't need?
   a Stop buying things like chocolate and cheese.
   b Be careful not to buy food you will waste.
   c Write down everything you want to buy.

3 Why are avocados expensive in London?
   a It costs a lot to get them to the UK.
   b They are rare in UK stores.
   c Not enough people want to buy them.

4 What reasons does the article give for buying lentils?
   a They are cheap, healthy, and don't make you fat.
   b They taste good and are filling.
   c You can use them instead of meat.

5 What kind of people go on survival vacations?
   a People who want to get free meat.
   b People who know a lot about collecting food from the wild.
   c People who usually live in cities and work in offices.

6 Why can it be dangerous to collect food from the countryside?
   a It's not easy to know which seaweed you can eat.
   b You could easily get lost.
   c Some plants are poisonous.

7 Why do you need to be careful with special offers?
   a The quality of the food may not be very high.
   b They may encourage you to buy more than you can use.
   c The food may sometimes be rotten.

3 Find the five examples of *one* or *ones* in the text. Write the nouns that they substitute.

1 _____   4 _____
2 _____   5 _____
3 _____

GRAMMAR: *-ing* forms and infinitives

1 Complete the sentences with the correct form of the verbs in parentheses.

1 It's cheaper (travel) _____ coach class on the train.
2 Is Phil good at (play) _____ the piano?
3 Lara was looking forward to (visit) _____ her cousin.
4 I'll call Joe when we've finished (eat) _____ dinner.
5 Anna plans to go to Australia (do) _____ some sightseeing.
6 I don't mind (pay) _____ for your train ticket.
7 I'm not sure what time you want (leave) _____ this evening?
8 Allan asked me (carry) _____ his suitcase.
9 Sylvia doesn't feel like (go out) _____. She has a bad headache.
10 (Run) _____ is really hard for me. I have bad knees.

2 Complete the sentences with the correct form of the verbs in the box.

> forget   meet   not wake   come   find   not have
> not make   fly   swim   invite   see   call

1 We looked everywhere _____ the perfect present for Valeria.
2 I'm nervous about the trip abroad because I'm scared of _____.
3 Alice was asleep, and we decided _____ her.
4 _____ is a great form of exercise.
5 I'm thinking of _____ Nigel to my birthday party.
6 I forgot my phone. I hate _____ it with me.
7 Mavis is in such good shape it's easy _____ that she's almost 90.
8 We told the children _____ too much noise.
9 _____ new people is exciting.
10 We asked her to join us in the park, but she refused _____.
11 The doctor told Graham _____ him on his cell-phone number.
12 I recommend _____ the city at night. The lights are amazing.

VOCABULARY: Eating out

3 Complete 1–3 with the words in the box.

> bowl   fork   knife   medium   pepper
> plate   rare   salt   spoon   vinegar
> well-done

1 things that add flavor to food
_____ _____ _____

2 things used for serving and eating food
_____ _____ _____
_____ _____

3 ways to describe how long meat is cooked for
_____ _____ _____

4 Complete the words.

1 It's getting late. Let's ask the waiter for the _____k and pay.
2 I like quiet restaurants, but my boyfriend prefers somewhere with a more lively a_____e.
3 Shrimp curry sounds nice. I think I'll _____r that.
4 He finished eating and wiped his mouth with a _____in.
5 It's a popular restaurant – I think we should _____e a table.
6 I was so embarrassed when I spilt coffee all over the clean white _____e_____h!
7 The waiter was very helpful, so we left him a big _____p.
8 Our meal took two hours to come. The _____e was so slow.

PRONUNCIATION: *-ing*

5 ▶ 9.2 Listen to the sentences. Are the *-ing* syllables pronounced as /ɪŋ/ or /ɪn/? Listen again and repeat.

1	Reading is my main hobby.	/ɪŋ/	/ɪn/
2	I really miss talking to Jenny.	/ɪŋ/	/ɪn/
3	We went skiing in Austria.	/ɪŋ/	/ɪn/
4	I recommend reserving a table.	/ɪŋ/	/ɪn/
5	I'm playing tennis with Sam.	/ɪŋ/	/ɪn/
6	I love having friends over for a meal.	/ɪŋ/	/ɪn/

SPEAKING: Making and responding to suggestions

1 ▶9.3 Listen to the conversations between Kris, Hannah, and Aidan. Check (✓) the correct name or names.

	Kris	Hannah	Aidan
1 Who suggests going for pizza?			
2 Who has already had pizza today?			
3 Who has never been to the Mexican restaurant before?			
4 Who can't eat shrimp?			
5 Who asks for an opinion about the zucchini?			
6 Who enjoyed the zucchini?			
7 Who wanted to leave the biggest tip?			
8 Who tried to persuade Kris to leave a bigger tip?			
9 Who liked the waitress?			
10 Who changed his or her mind about the tip?			

2 ▶9.3 Listen again and check (✓) the phrases you hear. Write M if they are for making a suggestion, P for responding positively, and N for responding negatively.

1 Should we ... _____ _____
2 That sounds great. _____ _____
3 Well, I'm not sure. _____ _____
4 To be honest, I'd rather ... _____ _____
5 Of course. _____ _____
6 Great idea! _____ _____
7 I suggest we ... _____ _____
8 Yes, let's. _____ _____
9 I won't have any, if that's OK. _____ _____
10 Why don't you ... ? _____ _____
11 I was wondering if we could ... _____ _____
12 Can't we ..., instead? _____ _____

3 Use your own ideas and some of the phrases in exercise 2 to complete these conversations.

1 Two friends are deciding what to do on a day off.
   A (Make a suggestion) _____
   B (Give a negative response and suggest something different) _____
   A (Try to persuade B to change his/her mind)
   _____
   B (Agree to A's suggestion) _____

2 Two friends are discussing a movie they have both seen.
   A (Ask for B's opinion on the movie)
   _____
   B (Give an opinion) _____
   A (Disagree with B's opinion and give reasons)
   _____
   B (Say you do not agree with A)
   _____

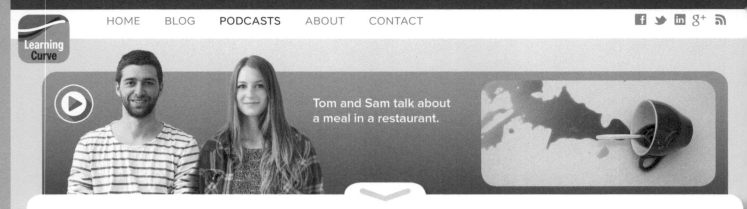

HOME   BLOG   PODCASTS   ABOUT   CONTACT

Tom and Sam talk about a meal in a restaurant.

LISTENING

1 ▶ 9.4 Listen to the podcast and number a–f in the order that they are mentioned (1–6).

a an accident involving a cup of coffee   _____

b how long the meat had been cooked   _____

c an argument about the table they had reserved   _____

d the table that Gabriel and his girlfriend were given   _____

e the appearance of the restaurant   _____

f how long they had to wait for their food   _____

2 ▶ 9.4 Listen again and complete the sentences with one or two words.

1 Sam reminded Tom that he had some _____ while he was working as a waiter.

2 The waiter said that Gabriel had asked for a table for _____ people.

3 Gabriel asked for a table by _____.

4 Gabriel and his girlfriend were given a table near the _____ the restaurant.

5 Gabriel said that the waiter was _____ to them.

6 Their food took a long time to _____.

7 Gabriel's girlfriend ordered a rare _____.

8 The service was not very good, so Gabriel did not leave _____.

READING

1 Read Jack's blog on page 55 and check (✔) the things he mentions.

a his views on different diets, such as vegetarianism and veganism   _____

b how many dishes he is prepared to cook   _____

c the kind of food he especially likes eating   _____

d the fact that one of his friends is trying to lose weight   _____

e the place where he is going to have his dinner party   _____

2 Does Jack say these things in his blog? Circle Yes (Y) or No (N).

1 He is worried that he is getting old.   Y / N

2 He wants to celebrate other things in addition to his birthday.   Y / N

3 Two of his guests have decided to get married.   Y / N

4 Five of his guests do not eat meat.   Y / N

5 Two of his guests have problems with their health when they eat certain foods.   Y / N

6 One of his guests has recently changed his/her diet.   Y / N

7 Apart from the engaged couple, none of his guests know each other.   Y / N

8 The menus have to include suggestions for drinks.   Y / N

9 There will be rewards for the best menus.   Y / N

10 He is hoping that his readers will create different and surprising menus.   Y / N

3 Make a list of all the food items mentioned in the text.

HOME   **BLOG**   PODCASTS   ABOUT   CONTACT

Guest blogger Jack writes about a special dinner party.

Cooking challenge

Cooking for friends is one of life's great pleasures. (I know, I would say that – I'm a chef!) So, to celebrate my birthday this year – the big three-oh – I've decided to make dinner for ten of my closest friends. I'd like to make this a really special evening, for several reasons.

One of my guests has just returned from three years in Australia, two other friends have recently gotten engaged and another – my oldest and dearest friend – has just been promoted at work. Life is good, and we're in the mood for celebrating! However, this is a slightly different kind of dinner party, because my *fabulous* friends have very particular (and very varied) food requirements. They are as follows:

- **Guest no. 1** is a strict vegetarian, but hates eating garlic. (I mean, really hates it and can taste it in the *tiniest* quantities!)

- **Guest no. 2** is also a vegetarian, but can't eat nuts of any kind. They make her sick. Oh, and she *really* doesn't like avocados. (How can anyone not like avocados?)

- **Guest no. 3** has recently turned vegan (so absolutely no animal products, including milk, eggs, yogurt, etc.) Also, he's not fond of soy sauce or other soya products.

- **Guest no. 4** doesn't eat meat, but is fine with fish (but not shellfish).

- **Guest no. 5** is on a diet so, if possible, would like to avoid cheese, desserts, and fried foods.

- **Guest no. 6** is allergic to citrus fruit, so absolutely no oranges, lemons or limes.

- **Guest no. 7** likes meat and pretty much nothing else. (Strangely, his best friend is guest no. 3!)

- **Guests 8, 9, 10** eat everything, in large quantities!

So, readers, I've decided to give you a challenge! Now that you've been presented with this long list of requirements and preferences, what would your menu look like? It has to include a starter, a main course, and a dessert. Guests will serve themselves from dishes set on the table. I'm happy to cook two dishes for each course – perhaps three for the main course – in order to provide options that everyone can enjoy.

Oh, and the first prize is dinner for four at The Goode Food Restaurant at any time this year. The second prize is dinner for two! There'll be extra points for original and unusual ideas! Get busy planning your menus, folks!

Right and wrong

10A — **LANGUAGE**

GRAMMAR: Reported speech

1 Choose the correct options to complete the sentences.

1 "I can't swim." Max told me he *won't be able to / couldn't / cannot* swim.

2 "I'll give you $10." Carrie said she would give *her / you / me* $10.

3 "Do you like running?" Gary asked me *if I liked / did I like / if I had liked* running.

4 "What have you done with the money?" They asked me what *did I do / had I done / I had done* with the money.

5 "James is broke." Dan *told me / told to me / told* that James was broke.

6 "You should resign." Milo said that I *should resign / should have resigned / had resigned*.

7 "I'm working hard." Juliet said that she *worked / was working / had worked* hard.

8 "You could try calling." He said that I *could have tried / could try / try* calling.

2 Read the things that your friend said. Then, complete the reported speech sentences with the correct information.

"I'm feeling nervous about my exam."

"I saw Mr. Jones last week."

"Have you visited Ged recently?"

"I can't remember Maria's address."

"Why did you go to Paris?"

"Are you happy in college?"

1 **A** Is she ready for her exam?
B I'm not sure. She said she _____ nervous about it.

2 **A** Did she mention Mr. Jones?
B Yes, she said she _____ last week.

3 **A** Did she ask you anything about Ged?
B Yes, she asked me _____ him recently.

4 **A** Did she give you Maria's address?
B No, she said she _____ it.

5 **A** Did she ask you about Paris?
B Yes, she asked me why I _____ there.

6 **A** Did she ask you about college?
B Yes, she asked me _____ happy.

VOCABULARY: Crime

3 Read the statements and check (✔) True or False.

		True	False
1	A mugging usually takes place in someone's home.	True	False
2	People sometimes have to pay a fine for a crime that is not very serious.	True	False
3	A burglar usually steals money from a bank.	True	False
4	If something is against the law, you may be punished if you do it.	True	False
5	"Theft" is a general word for the crime of stealing things.	True	False
6	Someone who has been killed is called a murderer.	True	False
7	It is possible to mug someone without that person realizing a crime has taken place.	True	False
8	A thief is someone who has taken something that belongs to someone else.	True	False

4 Complete the newspaper articles with crime words.

Police are looking for a man after a ¹b_____ at the home of a wealthy city art dealer last week. He ²b_____ into the house through a back window while the owner was out and ³s_____ jewelry and paintings worth several thousand dollars. The ⁴s_____, described by a ⁵w_____ who saw him running to a getaway car, is a slim man with dark hair.

A woman has appeared in ⁶c_____, accused of ⁷m_____ after a body was discovered in a house in Brooklyn. Police ⁸a_____ her after finding photographs of the ⁹v_____ in her apartment. If she is found guilty, she is likely to spend years in ¹⁰p_____.

PRONUNCIATION: Sentence stress

5 ▶10.1 Listen to the sentences. Are the <u>underlined</u> words stressed (S) or unstressed (U)? Listen again and repeat.

1 Liam said <u>that</u> he was tired. _____

2 I asked them <u>why</u> they were laughing. _____

3 Hannah asked <u>if</u> I wanted a drink. _____

4 Tom asked me <u>where</u> to go. _____

5 Petra asked me <u>who</u> I'd told. _____

6 They told her <u>why</u> they were angry. _____

LISTENING: Listening in detail

1 (▶)10.2 Alex and Lucy are talking about crimes. <u>Underline</u> the key words in the questions and options. Then listen and choose the correct options.

1 Why isn't Lucy feeling very happy?
a Thieves stole things from her house.
b Someone damaged the glass in her back door.
c Burglars came into her house and woke her up.

2 What was Lucy doing while the incident was happening?
a She was walking around upstairs.
b She was listening to the people downstairs.
c She was in bed.

3 What was taken from Lucy's house?
a Her watch, laptop, phone, and car keys.
b James's watch, laptop, phone, and car keys.
c James's watch and laptop, Lucy's phone, and the car keys.

4 What happened to Alex's neighbor, Karen?
a She had a nightmare.
b She was robbed on the street.
c A burglar stole her necklace.

5 Why was Karen's necklace special?
a Her husband gave it to her when they got married.
b It was worth a lot of money.
c It was a birthday present from her husband.

6 Who saw what happened to Karen?
a a man riding a bike
b someone in a car
c a witness walking nearby

7 What happened to the criminal Alex is telling Lucy about?
a He was arrested and gave the necklace back.
b He was arrested and sent to prison.
c He was arrested and has to go to court.

8 Lucy would feel better if
a the burglars hadn't stolen her phone.
b the police had found her car.
c the burglars had been arrested.

2 (▶)10.2 Choose the correct options to complete these sentences. Listen again if you need to.

1 The glass in Lucy's back door *was / wasn't* broken by the burglars.

2 The burglars only stole things from *upstairs / downstairs*.

3 The thieves stole Lucy's *phone / laptop*.

4 Alex's neighbor was robbed by a *burglar / mugger*.

5 Karen's necklace was a *birthday / wedding* present.

6 The attack on Karen was seen by a witness who was *walking / driving* by.

7 Alex doesn't know if Karen's attacker will go to *prison / court*.

8 Lucy can't *sleep / relax* in her house because of the burglary.

3 (▶)10.3 Find words that end with /t/ and /d/ sounds in sentences 1–6. Write _ if they are linked to the next sound and circle them if they are not pronounced. Listen, check, and repeat.

1 My neighbor was mugged at three o'clock in the afternoon.

2 It had been her wedding present from her husband.

3 Someone driving by saw what was happening.

4 He has to go to court next week.

5 It happened so fast there was nothing she could do.

6 The man was arrested and sent to prison.

4 Complete the sentences with nouns made from the verbs in the box. There are three extra verbs.

achieve   review   argue   educate   disappoint
inform   imagine   decide   organize   govern
confuse   connect   protect

1 There was some _____ about the date of the meeting: Rob thought it was the 2nd, but Emma said it was the 4th.

2 They planted a row of trees to provide some _____ from the strong winds.

3 Maria continued her _____ at an art college in Japan.

4 There is a strong _____ between physical and emotional health.

5 The company was losing money, so we made the _____ to close it.

6 Winning an Oscar is an incredible _____.

7 Hans went online to find _____ about careers in fashion.

8 The children's stories showed a lot of _____.

9 We could see Olga's _____ when she failed to win the competition.

10 Seb and Georgie were having an _____ about who should wash the dishes.

GRAMMAR: Second conditional, *would*, *could*, *might*

1 Complete the sentences with the first or second conditional form of the verbs in parentheses.

1 If Sima _____ (start) a new hobby, she wouldn't be so bored.
2 I'm sure Yvette _____ (help) with the housework if Robin asked her to.
3 If Kazuo _____ (sell) all his paintings, he'd be able to buy a motorcycle.
4 We can go skiing if it _____ (snow).
5 If Max _____ (bring) some money, we can buy ice cream.
6 We _____ (have) a lot of problems if the machine broke.
7 If Alicia _____ (sell) her apartment, she won't have anywhere to live.
8 Pavel _____ (cook) dinner if you ask him to.

2 Complete the conversation with the correct form of the verbs in the box.

Leo	I wish you were coming on vacation with us, Greta. It would be much more fun if you ¹_____ there.
Greta	I'd come if I ²_____ more money, but I can't afford it.
Leo	You'd be able to afford it if you ³_____ so much on clothes.
Greta	It's my job that's the problem, not my clothes! If my employer ⁴_____ me more, it ⁵_____ so difficult to save money.
Leo	You could save more if you ⁶_____ your own meals instead of eating out all the time.
Greta	But you know I hate cooking!
Leo	Or if you ⁷_____ your bike, instead of taking cabs everywhere.
Greta	And you know I don't like bike riding, either.
Leo	All I'm saying is that if you ⁸_____ so much money, you ⁹_____ to come on vacation with us.
Greta	Well I might try a bit harder if you ¹⁰_____ me so much!

be able	pay	not criticize	not waste
be	cook	not spend	not be	have	ride

3 Complete the conversations with second conditional sentences. Use the underlined verbs and the verbs in parentheses.

1 A Should we take a cab?
   B No, if we _____ a cab, it _____ (be) too expensive.
2 A Is your little brother coming to the party?
   B No, if he _____, I _____ (have to) look after him the whole time.
3 A Are you going to take the bus?
   B No, if I _____ the bus, I _____ (not arrive) in time.
4 A Should we go swimming?
   B No, if we _____ swimming, we _____ (miss) the soccer game on TV.
5 A Is Carla going to enter the competition?
   B No, she knows she _____ (not win) if she _____ it.
6 A Should we ask Bernie to come to the movies with us?
   B No, even if we _____ him, he _____ (not come).
7 A Are you going to buy that car you told me about?
   B No, I _____ (not have) any money left if I _____ it.
8 A Do you think we should tell Anna what Dan said?
   B No, if we _____ her, she _____ (be) very upset.

PRONUNCIATION: Conditionals

4 ▶10.4 Listen to the sentences. Write 1 for first conditionals and 2 for second conditionals. Listen again, check, and repeat.

1 ____
2 ____
3 ____
4 ____
5 ____
6 ____
7 ____
8 ____

WRITING: Writing a for-and-against essay

ONLY DANGEROUS CRIMINALS SHOULD GO TO PRISON. DISCUSS.

(A) However, one disadvantage is the cost. 1_____ Sending people to prison can also have a very bad effect on their families, particularly if they have children. Moreover, prison can sometimes make people more likely to commit crimes in the future because they are influenced by other criminals that they meet there.

(B) Many countries have problems with their prison systems, and one of the major ones is that the prisons are often too full. 2_____ As a result, the prisoners do not have the chance to study or to gain work experience, which might help them lead better lives in the future. Therefore, some people think we should keep criminals who are not dangerous out of prisons and punish them in a different way.

(C) To sum up, I believe that we should only send people to prison if they are really dangerous. 3_____ However, I believe that we should find better methods of punishment, including ones that could have advantages for our society.

(D) The main advantage of sending criminals to prison is that it sends a clear message to society: if you commit a crime, you will be punished. 4_____ In addition, some crimes (for example, not paying large amounts of taxes) are not violent, but they are still very serious, and some people argue that people who commit these crimes should go to prison.

1 Read the for-and-against essay and number paragraphs A–D in the correct order 1–4.

1 _____   2 _____   3 _____   4 _____

2 Fill in blanks 1–4 in the essay with sentences a–f. There are two extra sentences.

a This does not mean that other criminals should not be punished.

b When this happens, staff cannot control the prisoners, and they spend most of their time in their cells.

c Children suffer when their parents are sent to prison.

d It is very expensive to keep someone in prison – as much as $60,000 a year in some states.

e I believe that anyone who commits murder should go to prison for life.

f Freedom is important to everyone and, if you know you could lose it, you might not commit a crime.

3 "It is impossible to be happy if you are poor. Discuss." Are these topic sentences arguments for (F) or against (A) the essay title?

1 The main advantage of having plenty of money is that it makes life less stressful. _____

2 To sum up, the love of your friends and family is the only thing that can really make you happy. _____

3 On the other hand, if you do not have much money, you will not have the chance to do as many interesting things in life. _____

4 However, one disadvantage of having a lot of money is that it can be difficult to know who your real friends are. _____

5 To sum up, happiness is difficult to achieve if you are always worrying about how to pay for the things you need. _____

6 On the one hand, it is certainly possible to have a lot of fun without spending much money. _____

4 Use your own ideas to complete topic sentences for the two essays.

1 "Cigarettes should be illegal. Discuss."

a The main advantage of

_____

b However, one disadvantage

_____

c To sum up,

_____

2 "Everyone should have the chance to go to college. Discuss."

a On the one hand,

_____

b On the other hand,

_____

c To sum up,

_____

5 Choose an essay title from exercise 3 or 4. Write a for-and-against essay.

• Write four paragraphs.

• Start each paragraph with a topic sentence, using ideas from exercise 3.

• Use a formal style.

HOME   BLOG   PODCASTS   ABOUT   CONTACT

Learning Curve

Tom and Sam talk about crime.

LISTENING

1 ▶ 10.5 Listen to the podcast and check (✔) the words that you hear.

a thieves _____
b steal _____
c victim _____
d arrest _____
e theft _____
f murders _____
g prison _____
h mugging _____
i burglaries _____
j robbery _____

2 ▶ 10.5 Listen again. Are the sentences true (T), false (F), or doesn't say (DS)?

1 Tom thinks that people's behavior is better these days. _____

2 Most people believe that we live in a better society than in the past. _____

3 Michael says that his family and friends are kind, honest people. _____

4 Thieves do not usually use the Internet to commit crime. _____

5 Tom has been a victim of online theft. _____

6 According to Michael, mugging is not a very serious crime. _____

7 In the area where Michael lives, there were more burglaries last year. _____

8 Michael's house was burglarized last year. _____

READING

1 Read Marc's blog on page 61 and check (✔) the things it says about the robber.

a He put pictures of himself with stolen money on Facebook. _____

b He stole a car after he robbed a Chase bank. _____

c He told friends about his plan to commit the crime before he did it. _____

d He used a different name on social media. _____

e He always used a gun when he robbed banks. _____

2 Choose the correct options to complete the sentences.

1 Marc admits that he does not know a lot about
   a social media.
   b movies.
   c criminals.

2 Using social media, Jesse Hippolite told his friends that he
   a had robbed a bank in New York.
   b planned to rob a bank in New York.
   c had robbed lots of banks in New York.

3 Someone helped the police by giving them information about Hippolite's
   a car.
   b social media account.
   c friends.

4 Hippolite's car
   a had been parked outside a bank that had been robbed.
   b had been parked outside many banks that had been robbed.
   c was in a picture he had posted on social media.

5 Willie Sutton
   a escaped from prison several times.
   b went to prison for 40 years.
   c was never sent to prison for his crimes.

6 Marc says the police believe Hippolite committed
   a three robberies.
   b sixteen robberies.
   c nineteen robberies.

Guest blogger Marc writes about an unfortunate criminal.

THE WORST CRIMINAL?

You know I like to use this blog to pass on stories that involve social media, especially ones that relate specifically to New York. Well, today I have an incredible one for you about a not-so-clever criminal called Jesse Hippolite.

Now, I'm no expert on criminal behavior, and perhaps I've watched a few too many gangster movies, but I'd always assumed that robbery was something that people did secretly. (You know, to avoid being arrested?) But this guy, who has apparently been responsible for robbing a large number of banks in the New York area, liked to do things differently. Last July, the 24-year-old bank robber told his friends on Facebook that he was going to rob a bank. He posted, "I Gotta Get that $$$$$ Man!!!!" on the social media site just an hour before he robbed a Chase bank in Brooklyn, New York. The young robber had also said on Facebook that crime "paid his bills," as well as posting several photographs of himself counting $100 bills for the camera.

And how was he found? Well, a witness to one of his robberies had written down Hippolite's license plate number and handed it to the police. So when the police were given his number, they used their CCTV camera system to check where his car had been parked during the previous weeks. It turned out that the car had been very near the scene of no less than nineteen different bank robberies. The police then examined the suspect's social media account (something the police often do now, apparently), and that told them all they needed to know.

The young criminal used the name Willie Sutton Jr. on his Facebook profile, the famous bank robber who, during his 40-year "career" from the 1920s to the 1950s, stole $2 million.

He spent over half of his life in prison, escaping no less than three times with the use of clever disguises.

Interestingly, Hippolite never used a gun in his robberies, preferring instead to hand over handwritten notes to bank staff that threatened: "GIVE ME ALL THE MONEY!!! $100s, $50s, $20s ONLY."

Hippolite, who was charged with committing three robberies and is a suspect in a further sixteen, admitted in court that he had carried out these crimes. He now faces a possible 60-year prison sentence. Should be plenty of time to regret his actions – and his stupidity!

The natural world

11A | **LANGUAGE**

GRAMMAR: Articles

1 Match the two parts of the sentences.

1 I think it's a _____
2 Luis Sylva is the _____
3 Ava and I met a _____
4 Danny and I watched an _____
5 You can't look at the _____
6 We can't just stay at _____
7 I love all his films, but this is the _____
8 We're excited because we're off to _____
9 My sister has always loved _____
10 On the way there, we flew over the _____

   a amazing documentary about space.
   b home all day!
   c animals.
   d Paris next week.
   e Atlantic Ocean.
   f very interesting woman at Lara's house.
   g sun directly.
   h really fascinating and original movie.
   i best one of all.
   j guy who we spoke to earlier.

2 Complete the sentences with the correct article or no article (–).

1 Sophie has always been terrified of _____ spiders.
2 He's studying Spanish, but _____ teacher's not very good.
3 I've always found history _____ really fascinating subject.
4 We're not sure what her job is. Perhaps she's _____ salesclerk.
5 Do you prefer _____ dogs or _____ cats?
6 It was a very beautiful hotel, but _____ service there was terrible.
7 What was _____ first country you ever visited?
8 He usually goes to _____ work around eight o'clock.
9 I have to admire _____ doctors. They do such a difficult job.
10 How many times _____ week do you cook at home?

VOCABULARY: The natural world

3 Complete the sentences with the words in the box.

> hail   hurricane   rainbow   tornado   monsoon
> sea   icebergs   earthquake   flood   hill

1 When the ground started to shake, I knew it was a(n) _____
2 There was a (n)_____ downtown after the banks of the local river burst.
3 We thought it was snow, but then realized it was _____.
4 Let's climb up the _____ to see the view over the town.
5 The _____ lasted almost two weeks, with winds reaching speeds of 180 miles an hour.
6 Melting _____ in these regions are causing sea levels to rise.
7 Look at that fantastic _____ in the sky!
8 Do you prefer the _____ or swimming pools?
9 I was there during the _____ season, so it was very wet.
10 They could see the _____ approaching – a spinning column of air.

4 Complete the words.

1 They're staying at a hotel on the c_____ of Thailand.
2 The Amazon Rainforest is a j_____ where more than 1,300 kinds of birds live.
3 Mount Vesuvius is an active v_____ in southern Italy. It last erupted in 1944.
4 Many of the trees in this f_____ have been cut down for fuel and building materials.
5 The world's largest hot d_____ is the Sahara in Africa.
6 If all the world's g_____ melted, sea levels would rise by about 70 meters.
7 She used to keep the horse in a f_____ behind her house.
8 Last night's huge s_____ brought wind and rain and destroyed many houses.

PRONUNCIATION: *the*

5 ▶11.1 Read the sentences. Is *the* pronounced /ðə/ or /ði:/? Listen, check, and repeat.

1 They live in the Arctic.	/ðə/	/ði:/
2 We made our way through the jungle.	/ðə/	/ði:/
3 The icebergs are surrounded by fog.	/ðə/	/ði:/
4 Have you seen the rainbow?	/ðə/	/ði:/
5 We swam in the ocean.	/ðə/	/ði:/
6 The earthquake destroyed a lot of buildings.	/ðə/	/ði:/
7 Why don't you drive along the coast?	/ðə/	/ði:/
8 Is the volcano still active?	/ðə/	/ði:/

READING: Understanding the writer's purpose

IF YOU CAN'T STAND THE HEAT …

When we think of sunshine, happy scenes of vacations and beaches usually spring to mind. [1]But what about places like Death Valley in California or the Sahara Desert? Here, the heat is far from being pleasant – in fact, it's downright dangerous.

[2]Our bodies function within a fairly narrow temperature range, and conditions that cause a rise in that temperature can be extremely serious. People suffering from heatstroke lose the ability to regulate their temperature. [3]This can lead to a range of symptoms from headaches and dizziness to heart and brain problems and sometimes death, all within an alarmingly short period of time.

Even people who have lived all their lives in hot countries can be affected. [4]In 2015, over 1,300 people died during a heatwave in Karachi. With temperatures of over 40°C, hospitals were totally overwhelmed by the number of people suffering from heat-related illnesses. Interestingly, scientists have discovered that around half of the Aboriginal people in Western Australia have a gene that helps them survive at higher temperatures. It is not yet known why people in other hot climates have not evolved in the same way.

Despite the great heat, some people are attracted to the idea of traveling in extremely hot places like deserts. [5]For such a trip, the most important thing is to take more water than you think you could possibly need. [6]In addition to being extremely hot, deserts can also be very tricky to navigate, with sand and dunes stretching for miles in every direction, and there are many cases of people getting lost in them with fatal results.

---

1 Read the text and choose the correct options, according to the information given.

1 Why isn't sunshine always a good thing?
   a If you're not on vacation, it can be unpleasant.
   b Some types of heat are especially bad.
   c Too much heat can harm you.

2 Are our bodies well adapted for heat and cold?
   a No, we can only deal with small changes in temperature.
   b Yes, if we take care to regulate our temperature.
   c No, our bodies need to stay at the same temperature.

3 Do people often die when they get heatstroke?
   a No, most people recover pretty quickly.
   b Not everyone – some people have more minor symptoms.
   c Yes, and it happens pretty quickly.

4 What is unusual about some Aboriginal people?
   a They have developed to function better than most people in hot weather.
   b They have a lot of knowledge about how to stay healthy in hot weather.
   c They are used to living in very hot places.

5 In what way does the landscape of deserts sometimes cause problems?
   a It is difficult to drive on sand.
   b Everything looks the same, so it is difficult to find the right direction.
   c There are no other people around to offer help.

2 Match sentences 1–6 in the text with purposes a–f.

a giving advice   _____
b describing a place   _____
c making a comparison or contrast   _____
d describing an event   _____
e explaining a cause or result   _____
f giving information or facts   _____

3 Underline the subject in these sentences. Is it a noun (N) or a noun phrase (NP)?

1 Thunder crashed in the sky above us.   _____
2 Homes that are built on cliff tops can collapse.   _____
3 The ship's path was blocked by icebergs.   _____
4 Steep wooded hills provide shelter for the deer.   _____
5 For me, swimming is the perfect exercise.   _____
6 Everyone in the room started yelling at him.   _____

GRAMMAR: Third conditional

1 Choose the correct options to complete the sentences.

1 If you'd asked me, I _____ you.
   a would help   b would have helped
   c had helped

2 If they'd told us about the problem, Tom _____ it for them.
   a could have fixed   b could fix
   c had fixed

3 I would have called you if I _____ in trouble.
   a know you are   b knew you were
   c had known you were

4 If we'd taken the earlier flight, we _____ plenty of time.
   a would have   b would have had
   c have had

5 Lucy might have been upset if she _____ the truth about her boyfriend.
   a had known   b knew
   c knows

6 If I hadn't been sick, I would _____ to work.
   a go   b have gone
   c gone

7 I may not have been so angry if she _____ at me in front of everyone.
   a didn't yell   b doesn't yell
   c hadn't yelled

8 You wouldn't have had the accident if you _____ so careless!
   a hadn't been   b aren't
   c weren't

2 Complete the third conditional sentences with the verbs in parentheses in the correct order.

1 If Luis _____ attention, he _____ the instructions. (pay/understand)

2 I _____ a card if you _____ me it was her birthday. (send/tell)

3 Mira _____ earlier if she _____ the train. (take/arrive)

4 I _____ to the party if they _____ me. (invite/go)

5 If you _____ us, we _____ to the meeting. (not go/warn)

6 If it _____, the fair _____ a success. (not rain/be)

7 They _____ wet if they _____ umbrellas. (not get/take)

8 We _____ lost if you _____ to my directions! (listen/not be)

VOCABULARY: Extreme adjectives

3 Choose the correct adjectives to complete the sentences.

1 My friend Karina really makes me laugh – she's *starving / hilarious / miserable*.

2 She hated living on her own. It made her really *filthy / freezing / miserable*.

3 What a big car – it's *exhausted / enormous / hilarious*!

4 Turn the heat down – it's *freezing / boiling / furious*!

5 Our vacation couldn't have been better – it was *fantastic / furious / enormous*!

6 I was *hilarious / tiny / furious* because he'd been rude to me.

4 Complete the conversation with the correct adjectives.

Paulo So tell me about your vacation. Was it fun?

Yekta Yes and no. I hadn't realized how cold it would be at this time of year – it was ¹f_____! The hotel wasn't great, either. Our room looked so big on the website, but, actually, it was ²t_____. And it wasn't very clean. In fact, the bathroom was ³f_____. I had to ask them to clean it before I could use it.

Paulo What about the food? What was that like?

Yekta Well, it was OK, but there wasn't enough. Two hours after eating, we were both ⁴s_____!

Paulo And what about the town itself? Was that nice?

Yekta Yes, actually, it's full of beautiful old buildings, so it's really ⁵g_____. It's so incredible to look at. I have some great photos to show you.

Paulo Great! So did you spend most of your time looking around?

Yekta Yes, in fact, we walked so much on the first day, by the evening, we were both ⁶e_____.

PRONUNCIATION: Weak form of *have*

5 ▶11.2 Practice saying the sentences. Remember to pronounce the vowel sound in *have* as /əv/. Listen, check, and repeat.

1 If you'd gotten the bus, you wouldn't have been so late.

2 She would have paid less if she'd followed my advice.

3 He wouldn't have been so tired if he'd gone to bed earlier.

4 If I'd stayed longer, I might have seen Lily.

5 They might not have gotten lost if they'd listened to John.

6 She would have impressed me more if she hadn't been so rude!

7 If she'd taken some money, she could have bought some lunch.

8 If they'd listened to me, they wouldn't have made this mistake.

SPEAKING: Making recommendations

1 ▶11.3 Mimi is talking about her travel plans with her friends Salma and Jack. Before you listen, try to complete the phrases they use for asking for ideas or making recommendations. Then listen and check.

1 Where _____ the best place to go?

2 Perhaps _____ get one of those round-the-world flights.

3 Do you have _____ about the best countries to visit?

4 I _____ going there in the monsoon season.

5 You _____ go to the Kiso Valley – it's gorgeous.

6 But if I _____, I'd keep my shoes and clothes near my bed.

2 ▶11.4 Read the conversation and complete 1–5 with a–e. Listen and check.

A I have 24 hours in New York on my way to Mexico. What do you think I should do while I'm there?

B You should definitely go on the Staten Island ferry.

A ¹_____

B Yes it is, and you get great views of the Manhattan skyline.

A ²_____

B If the weather's nice, I'd recommend getting a picnic from a deli.

A ³_____

B You know, somewhere you can buy bread, sandwich meats, cheese, fruit, that sort of thing. There are plenty of delis in New York.

A ⁴_____

B Yes, but only if the sun's shining! And of course, you really have to walk across Brooklyn Bridge.

A ⁵_____

B A Broadway show, of course!

a So what you're saying is that I should buy some food and then find a park to eat it in.

b Oh, OK. It's free, isn't it?

c That sounds like fun. And what would you recommend doing in the evening?

d And where would be the best place to get lunch?

e I'm sorry. I'm not sure I've understood what you meant.

3 Complete the tag questions.

1 You can buy tickets in advance, _____?

2 The bus leaves from over there, _____?

3 It's the highest mountain in Latin America, _____?

4 You've been to Fiji, _____?

5 The weather won't be too bad, _____?

6 Clara recommended this hotel, _____?

4 Use your own words to summarize the advice given. The first one is done for you.

1 You can get a cheaper cab, but they're not always safe. You should always get an official one, even if you have to wait longer for it.
So what you're saying is that I need to get an official cab.

2 This restaurant is famous for its lamb dishes. The meat they use is all from local farms. I know you usually prefer seafood, but remember that we're a long way from the sea here, so it won't be very fresh.
So what you're saying is _____.

3 You can buy tickets at any of the tourist attractions. However, I'd recommend buying a tourist pass because then you can get into all the main museums, in addition to going on as many buses as you'd like, so it's really reasonable.
So what you're saying is _____.

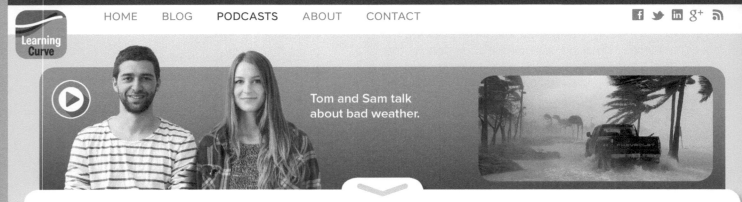

HOME   BLOG   PODCASTS   ABOUT   CONTACT

Tom and Sam talk about bad weather.

LISTENING

1 ▶ 11.5 Listen to the podcast and check (✔) the words that you hear.

a   hurricane   _____

b   rainbow   _____

c   coast   _____

d   tornado   _____

e   sea   _____

f   hail   _____

g   monsoon   _____

h   flood   _____

i   storm   _____

2 ▶ 11.5 Listen again. Complete the sentences with one or two words.

1   Bad weather is stopping a lot of tourists from going _____.

2   _____ once prevented Tom from leaving New York.

3   Isabella was staying in Florida when there was _____.

4   Isabella couldn't walk outside because it was so _____.

5   The people working in the hotel told the guests to stay _____.

6   Isabella thought _____ was like a monsoon.

7   When the hurricane finally stopped, Isabella had been in the hotel for _____.

8   Lots of _____ fell down because of the hurricane.

READING

1 Read Kate's blog on page 67 and number a–e in the order she mentions them (1–5).

a   the features of a glacier   _____

b   a suggestion to the readers of the blog   _____

c   why she was worried about the helicopter flight _____

d   an alternative to a heli-hike   _____

e   how they traveled to the glacier   _____

2 Check (✔) the correct sentences.

1   Kate feels she just had a very special experience.   _____

2   She is sure that she can describe how fantastic the experience was.   _____

3   Before the helicopter flight, Kate had told Sophie that she was worried about it. _____

4   The helicopter flight was actually more comfortable than a plane flight.   _____

5   The helicopter landed on the highest part of the glacier.   _____

6   They stopped briefly before beginning the glacier walk.   _____

7   The surface of the glacier was completely flat.   _____

8   Heli-hikes only take place if the weather is good.   _____

3 Find ten examples of extreme adjectives in the text.

Guest blogger Kate writes about an amazing experience.

On top of the world

Yesterday, Sophie and I had the experience of a lifetime here in New Zealand – a day's "heli-hike" on the indescribably beautiful Franz Josef glacier. How can I possibly explain to you how spectacular it was? Since pictures sometimes speak louder than words, perhaps I'll start with a photo:

We arrived on the glacier after the most thrilling helicopter flight imaginable over the kind of landscape I'd only seen in nature shows: snow-capped mountain peaks and thick, dark forest. Beautiful! I'd been a little nervous about that helicopter flight. (Just ask Sophie!) An anxious flyer in the best of times, I'd had nightmares the previous night about falling out of the open door of the helicopter. In fact, after we had taken off (which was weird – that vertical lift!), it was no scarier than being on a normal plane. In fact it was probably a little smoother. And I had the incredible scenery to distract me. Twenty amazing minutes later, our helicopter landed at the bottom of two icefalls, which are like frozen waterfalls, and we all got out. After a ten-minute pause to admire the fantastic scenery, we started our three-hour glacier hike, led by the marvelous Daniel. (He was the perfect guide: friendly, full of interesting facts, and so much fun!) We hiked past enormous towers of ice (like something out of a fairy tale) and stood on the edge of deep, seemingly bottomless holes, which Daniel told us are called *moulins*. And, best of all, we saw gorgeous, sparkling blue ice. (Yes, ice as blue as the sky!)

We arrived back at our hotel completely exhausted last night. Both of us were so tired that we slept for ten hours without waking up once. And this morning we were starving – our breakfast had never tasted so good!

As long as I live, I feel I'll remember this trip. We were incredibly lucky with the weather – nice and warm with sunny, cloudless skies. If the trip had been canceled because of bad weather, the tour company would have arranged for us to do a glacier valley walk, instead. I'm sure it would have been great, but nothing like this. To anyone considering a glacier hike at any point in their life, I say *just do it*. You won't regret it.

One of Sophie's. (Her camera's better than mine, and if I'm honest, so are her camera skills!)

GRAMMAR: *So/Neither do I*

1 Choose the best options to complete the replies.

1 I can eat a whole bag of that candy.
   a So can I.   **b** So do I.
   c So will I.

2 I'm not going to the concert.
   a Neither do I.   **b** So am I.
   c Neither am I.

3 I don't eat meat.
   a Neither am I.   **b** Neither do I.
   c So do I.

4 I don't like snow.
   a Really? I do.   **b** Really? I have.
   c Really? I didn't.

5 One day I'd love to travel the world.
   a So do I.   **b** So am I.
   c So would I.

6 I haven't seen Maria in ages.
   a Neither have I.   **b** So have I.
   c Neither do I.

7 We won't be able to go tonight.
   a Neither do I.   **b** Neither have I.
   c Neither will I.

8 I go to work on Saturdays.
   a So have I.   **b** So do I.
   c So am I.

2 Read the sentences and complete the replies.

1 **A** I've seen that movie twice.
   B So _____ I!

2 **A** I'm afraid I won't be free this weekend.
   B Neither _____ I.

3 **A** I don't like mornings.
   B Really? I _____. It's the best time of the day for me!

4 **A** James hates being late.
   B So _____ Ali.

5 **A** If I'm tired, I can sleep in till noon.
   B So _____ my brother.

6 **A** I don't trust that man.
   B Neither _____ I!

7 **A** I've never been to Italy.
   B Actually, neither _____ I.

8 **A** I'd love to live in Paris for a year.
   B So _____ I.

9 **A** I haven't spent any money this week.
   B Really? I _____! I bought a new phone yesterday.

VOCABULARY: Phrases with *go* and *get*

3 Match the meaning of *get* in sentences 1–10 with the verbs in a–e.

1 I'm getting really excited about our vacation.   _____

2 Could you get me a book from the office, please?   _____

3 Did you get my text this morning?   _____

4 Great pants! Where did you get them?   _____

5 We got to the airport an hour before our flight.   _____

6 Jamie's just getting a blanket from the car.   _____

7 I got a really nice rug from that new Swedish store.   _____

8 It's getting cold, isn't it?   _____

9 Have you ever gotten a prize in a competition?   _____

10 She won't get to the concert on time tonight.   _____

   a We received some complaints about the program.

   b Everyone became pretty angry about the situation.

   c We arrived at the station just before eight o'clock.

   d I always buy a few souvenirs while I'm on vacation.

   e Should I bring in dinner yet?

4 Complete the conversation with one word in each blank to complete the expressions.

Finn You ¹_____ away last month, didn't you, Anna?

Anna I did, yeah. I'm ²_____ away to college this September, so my parents thought we should all go ³_____ vacation before I leave home.

Finn So where did you go?

Anna We went to New Zealand. The first week we went scuba ⁴_____ north of Auckland. And we went ⁵_____ some beautiful walks in the mountains.

Finn Did you get to Wellington?

Anna Yeah, we ⁶_____ a trip to the south of the island the second week and took a guided ⁷_____ of Wellington. It was gorgeous. What about you? Have you ⁸_____ anywhere exciting this year?

Finn Nothing as good as that!

PRONUNCIATION: Auxiliary verbs and stress

5 ▶ 12.1 Read the sentences and replies. <u>Underline</u> the syllables in the replies that you think will be stressed. Listen, check, and repeat.

1 "Be careful!" "I will."

2 "I feel tired." "So do I."

3 "I don't know." "Neither do I."

4 "I passed the exam." "So did I."

5 "I've finished lunch." "I haven't."

6 "I have a cold." "So do I."

LISTENING: Identifying agreement between speakers

1 ▶12.2 Listen to Neha and Lukas talking about vacations. Do they agree (A) or disagree (D) about 1–8?

		Agree	Disagree
1	Corsica is a beautiful island.		
2	It's nice to have very hot weather.		
3	It's best to go on vacation with other people.		
4	It's best to go on vacation with friends.		
5	Corsica has good hiking trails.		
6	Active vacations are better than lazy ones.		
7	Scuba diving is fun.		
8	Going on vacation is enjoyable.		

2 ▶12.2 Listen again. Are the following statements true (T), false (F), or not mentioned (N)?

1 Neha prefers the temperature to be over 30 degrees. ____
2 Neha is going on a hiking vacation. ____
3 Neha will be camping when she is in Nepal. ____
4 Lukas's friends, Karl and Trudi, work in Amsterdam. ____
5 The GR20 walk in Corsica is difficult. ____
6 Lukas enjoys spending days on the beach. ____
7 Lukas's friends usually get up very late on vaction. ____
8 Lukas's friends will go scuba diving with him. ____

3 ▶12.3 Look at the short sentences. Will the links marked _ be pronounced /w/ or /y/? Listen, check, and repeat.

1 He_always walks. ____
2 They_argue all the time. ____
3 It's so_interesting. ____
4 He's too_out of shape. ____
5 Why_are you laughing? ____
6 How_is Lucy? ____
7 We have a few_apples. ____
8 It's by_a lake. ____

4 Complete the words.

1 I like to walk around during the flight, so I'd prefer an a____ ____ ____ ____ seat.
2 You can ask a flight a____ ____ ____ ____ ____ ____ ____ for a glass of water.
3 Which g____ ____ ____ does our flight leave from?
4 You are only allowed one c____ ____ ____ ____-____ ____ b____ ____ on the flight.
5 Can you see our flight on the d____ ____ ____ ____ ____ ____ ____ board yet?
6 We went to the check-in desk and were given our b____ ____ ____ ____ ____ ____ passes.
7 There are lots of stores and cafés in the d____ ____ ____ ____ ____ ____ ____ ____ L____ ____ ____ ____.
8 We have about half an hour before we L____ ____ ____ at JFK airport.
9 We had to take our shoes off when we went through s____ ____ ____ ____ ____ ____ ____.
10 The plane was unable to t____ ____ ____ o____ ____ because of bad weather.

GRAMMAR: Modals of deduction

1 Choose the correct options to complete the sentences or say if both are correct.

1 I keep seeing Miguel on Green Street. He _____ work near there.
   a can   b must

2 Of course, he _____ not even live here – he could just be visiting.
   a might   b may

3 I'm not sure if that's Gabriel's wife with him. It _____ be her.
   a could   b might

4 I can hear noises coming from the apartment, so someone definitely _____ be there.
   a must   b can

5 That girl is at least ten. Laura's daughter has just learned to walk, so it _____ be her.
   a can't   b might not

6 He looks exactly like Alfonso. It _____ be his twin brother.
   a can   b must

7 I thought he was French, but I guess I _____ be wrong.
   a could   b can

8 The woman in the photo is much younger than the man, so she _____ be his mother.
   a can't   b must

2 Complete the sentences with *must*, *might*, and *can't*.

1 When we met Jack, he was 80; that was years ago, so he _____ be very old by now.

2 I have no idea who that guy is. It _____ be Sofia's boyfriend because he's away.

3 I'm not sure if Rachel's here today. She _____ be.

4 Pedro's boss is bald. That man has loads of dark hair, so it _____ be him.

5 It's completely dark outside – it _____ be pretty late.

6 I don't know whether Alice is right about Carlos. She _____ be.

7 There's snow on the ground in the painting, so it _____ be winter.

8 You haven't eaten since breakfast. You _____ be hungry!

3 Complete the conversation with modal verbs. There may be more than one answer.

A Did I tell you I ran into Maria this morning?
B You did?
A Yeah, we talked for a little while. Do you think she's wealthy?
B She ¹_____ be. Apparently, she has three houses in London and two apartments in New York!
A But she looks young – she ²_____ be more than 30.
B I'm not sure. I think she ³_____ be 35.
A Anyway, I keep seeing her. Do you think she's working somewhere near by?
B I have no idea. I guess she ⁴_____ be – or she ⁵_____ be staying with her brother, Nico.
A Ah, I saw a woman who looked like Maria leaving a house on Elm Street yesterday. It ⁶_____ be her, then.
B It ⁷_____ be the same person – Nico has three sisters!

PRONUNCIATION: Sentence stress

4 ▶12.4 Underline the words that are stressed in these sentences. Listen, check and repeat.

1 She must be over twenty.

2 It can't be that late!

3 They might be stuck in traffic.

4 It could be her father, I suppose.

5 They must be on their way.

6 He can't be angry about it.

7 She might be listening to music.

8 They must be leaving.

WRITING: Writing a review

Luxury Bicycle Trip in the Loire Valley, France

My friend and I went on this vacation last month. We had expected that a vacation with the word "luxury" in the title would provide fantastic hotels and good food.

Sadly, we were extremely disappointed. The hotels were pleasant enough, but very basic. In fact, at one of them, we even had to share a bathroom with the couple in the next room! In addition, the bikes they gave us were in very poor condition, and the maps were so out of date that we kept getting lost and having to use the GPS on my phone!

Luckily, the scenery was absolutely gorgeous, and we loved being out in the fresh air. Overall, I think this vacation would be good for students or young people who don't mind basic accommodations. However, it's not really suitable for anyone wanting a luxurious break.

Pizzeria Italia

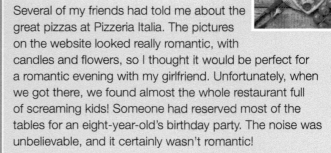

Several of my friends had told me about the great pizzas at Pizzeria Italia. The pictures on the website looked really romantic, with candles and flowers, so I thought it would be perfect for a romantic evening with my girlfriend. Unfortunately, when we got there, we found almost the whole restaurant full of screaming kids! Someone had reserved most of the tables for an eight-year-old's birthday party. The noise was unbelievable, and it certainly wasn't romantic!

Also, we had expected everything to be freshly made. However, our pizzas were rather hard and difficult to chew. Clearly, the bases had come out of the freezer. The cheese was OK, but there was far too much of it – my girlfriend couldn't finish hers.

When we complained, we were told that the usual chef was off sick. They offered us a free meal on another night. I think children might enjoy it, and I wouldn't mind taking my nieces and nephews (especially if it's free!), but I'm pretty sure my girlfriend wouldn't want to come!

1 Read the two reviews by Tom Green. Are the statements true (T) or false (F)?

Luxury Bicycle Trip

1 He thought they would have high-quality hotels and food. _____

2 The hotels and food were as good as he had expected. _____

3 The bikes that they were given for the trip were good. _____

4 They were able to follow the maps easily. _____

5 They enjoyed the views of the countryside. _____

6 He thinks young people would enjoy the vacation. _____

Pizzeria Italia

7 Some of his friends had said that the pizzas were excellent. _____

8 He thought the restaurant would be noisy. _____

9 He enjoyed being with lots of children. _____

10 The pizzas were not as good as he had expected. _____

11 He thinks the restaurant is good for a romantic evening out. _____

12 He plans to take his girlfriend there again. _____

2 Complete the sentences with the adverbs of attitude in the box or your own ideas. There may be more than one answer.

> surprisingly   hopefully   unfortunately
> sadly   clearly   obviously   luckily

1 The waiters all seemed very stressed out. _____, the restaurant needs more staff.

2 It was a beautiful day when we visited the national park. _____, there weren't many people there.

3 A sign offered two meals for the price of one. _____, they were trying to attract more customers.

4 We were unable to ski today because of the bad weather. _____, it will be better tomorrow.

5 This place specializes in Japanese food, but, _____, they don't serve sushi or sashimi.

6 I came to this resort five years ago and loved it. _____, several large hotels have been built since then, which has changed its character.

3 Think of a place you have been to on vacation. Write a review.

- Before you start, make notes about what was good and bad about it.
- Say what you were hoping for before you went there.
- Say what it was really like.
- Say what kind of people it would be best for.

Include at least two adverbs of attitude.

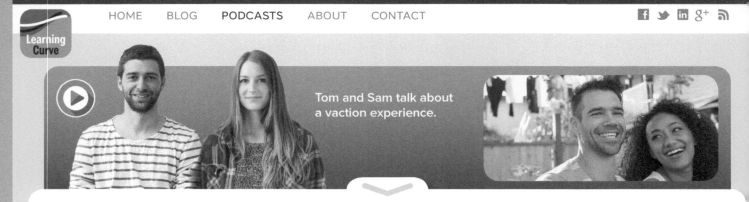

HOME   BLOG   PODCASTS   ABOUT   CONTACT

Tom and Sam talk about a vaction experience.

LISTENING

1 ▶ 12.5 Listen to the podcast and choose the correct options to complete the sentences.

1 Teresa likes going on vacation to places where
 a she can go hiking.
 b the countryside is beautiful.
 c there are fewer tourists.

2 While she was on vacation, Teresa met
 a a really interesting person.
 b someone that she knew from home.
 c the man who became her husband.

3 When Sam met someone she knew in Spain, they
 a went to the beach together.
 b had coffee together.
 c gave each other advice.

2 ▶ 12.5 Listen again. Are the statements true (T) or false (F)?

1 Teresa talks about a vacation in Spain. _____

2 Teresa saw someone she knew from home at the hotel. _____

3 The person she saw was a work colleague. _____

4 Teresa's husband did not believe that the person they had seen was Matthew. _____

5 Teresa and Matthew saw each other again during the vacation. _____

6 Sam enjoyed seeing someone she already knew on vacation. _____

READING

1 Read Simon's blog on page 73 and circle Y (Yes) if he says this or N (No) if he doesn't.

1 He never wants to travel by plane again. Y / N

2 He would be happier if people behaved differently in airports. Y / N

3 People get angry when he walks past them on the travelator. Y / N

4 He could not find anywhere to sit in Dulles airport. Y / N

5 People should not wear jewelry when traveling by plane. Y / N

2 Choose the correct options to complete the sentences.

1 Simon is irritated by
 a all aspects of traveling by plane.
 b passengers' behavior in the departure lounge.
 c passengers' behavior going through security.

2 Simon thinks people should
 a not look around them while they are on the travelator.
 b not use the travelator, but walk instead.
 c keep walking while they are on the travelator.

3 Simon says that in the departure lounge, he does not
 a sit in other people's seats.
 b sit next to people that he doesn't know.
 c put things on the seats next to him.

4 Simon says that some people do not realize that they
 a cannot take certain things in their luggage.
 b have to line up to go through security.
 c have to take off their clothes to go through security.

5 Simon says that people should
 a not forget to take their boarding passes.
 b keep their boarding passes safely in their hand luggage.
 c keep their boarding passes where they can quickly show them.

HOME **BLOG** PODCASTS ABOUT CONTACT

Guest blogger Simon writes about his experience flying.

THE PAIN OF PLANES

I think I might be doing a bit too much flying at the moment. I seem to find the whole experience annoying, from check-in to customs. And here, in no particular order, is why:

The travelator – you know, the moving floor. OK, this thing is designed to get us quickly to our destination. But we can always help it along by *using our legs*. Why do so many people choose to stand on the thing and just look around them? It's not like the view's so great. And, more to the point, why do they look so annoyed when they have to move to one side to allow people like myself to walk past them? Well, I'm sorry, people, but I HAVE A PLANE TO CATCH!

OK, so I'm in the departure lounge, trying to calmly read my book in between nervously checking the departure board. Apparently, my fellow passengers don't like sitting next to complete strangers. Well, neither do I, but if I have to now and then, it's really not the end of the world. So I don't put my bags, coats, or cups of coffee on the seat next to me to stop people from using the seats FOR THE PURPOSE FOR WHICH THEY WERE INTENDED-which is what everyone else seems to do. In Dulles airport in Washington D.C. yesterday, for example, there were people standing around with *nowhere* to sit, for goodness' sake, while the seats to the left and right of me were piled high with hand luggage!

Now why, after *all these years*, do some people *still* attempt to go through security with bottles of liquid, sharp objects, etc? And then they look astonished when these items are removed by the officials. Come *on*, people – you must know it's against the law by now! Oh, and while we're on the topic of security, if you know you're going to have to remove an item of clothing or a piece of jewelry, just do it BEFORE you reach the front of the line. Because it REALLY SLOWS THINGS DOWN WHEN YOU DON'T.

Oh, and boarding passes … don't get me started. You know you're going to have to show them to the flight attendant as you board the plane, so please have them *in your pocket*, and not buried somewhere in the bottom of your hand luggage!

Time to calm down! Think I'm going to go lie down in a darkened room for a while …

WRITING: Writing a report

How to become an actor

(1) _____

Anyone can stand on a stage and say a few words, but if you really want to act, you need to learn how to do it correctly. Take acting classes if you can afford them, or consider going to drama school. In addition, you should read books on acting techniques. But above all, watch the actors you love!

(2) _____

Everyone has to start somewhere, so don't be shy. Look for any possible chance to act and grab it with both hands! Even taking part in a school play is good experience. I also suggest trying your local theater – they often need extras for their plays. This will give you experience on stage, as well as the chance to learn about other aspects of an actor's life, such as scenery, costumes, and lighting.

(3) _____

You may be a good actor, but if you can ride a horse, ski, play an instrument, or dance, as well, this could give you an advantage. Therefore, remember to include all your skills on your résumé, even if you don't think they are very relevant.

(4) _____

Make sure people know about you. An attractive personal website is very important. In addition to this, networking is essential. If you know a lot of people in the business, you are more likely to get work. If possible, I would also recommend getting an agent. Agents usually have a great number of contacts and can help you get parts in movies and plays.

(5) _____

It's not surprising that most actors give up within a year. If you fail to get jobs, it can damage your confidence. Moreover, you need to keep paying rent even if you're not working! But if you are really serious, continue trying and keep believing that you will find success. One day you will!

1 Read the report and match paragraphs 1–5 with headings a–h. There are three extra headings.

a Study acting

b Everyone can act

c Start young

d The importance of experience

e Develop other skills

f Write a great résumé

g Tell people about yourself

h Don't stop trying!

2 Complete the sentences with the verbs in the box in the correct form.

> include get talk move visit keep

1 If you want a career in law, I suggest _____ to someone who already works as a lawyer.

2 Remember _____ your website up to date.

3 I recommend _____ several colleges before you decide on a progam.

4 For the best careers in finance, I suggest _____ to a big city, such as Hong Kong.

5 Before joining the army, I recommend _____ in the best shape that you can.

6 When you apply for a job, remember _____ an up-to-date résumé.

3 Complete these sentences with your own ideas.

1 Pilots must be physically healthy. In addition, _____.

2 To become a nurse, you will need good skills in maths and english, as well as _____.

3 Farmers need to be in shape and they have to be prepared to _____, as well.

4 Firefighters have to be prepared to work in dangerous situations. Moreover, _____.

5 If you own your own café, you often have to work very long hours. In addition to this, _____.

6 If you want to be an author, you should read as much as you can! In addition, _____.

4 Think of a job that you would like to do. Write a report on the best way to get that job. Use ideas from exercises 2 and 3 to help you.

- Plan four or five section headings.
- Include factual information.
- Make recommendations using *suggest*, *recommend*, and *remember*.

WRITING: For-and-against essays

In 2016, France became the first country to make it illegal for supermarkets to throw away unsold food. Should all countries do the same?

(A) _____ Some of them even put substances in their garbage bins so that the food cannot be eaten, even if it is still in good condition. This is to stop people from taking the food out of the bins. Many people believe that this is wrong, and that all countries should do the same as France. They should make supermarkets give their unsold food to charities so that they can give it to the poor people in our society who really need it.

(B) _____ After all, if supermarkets can't sell this food, it is better for charities to use it to feed the poor. Also, if a supermarket gives its unsold food to a charity, the people who work for the charity can make sure it is safe to eat. However, if people take food out of the garbage bins themselves, it could be dangerous to eat, and it might make them sick.

(C) _____ The supermarkets have paid for the food, so they should be able to decide what to do with it. In addition, if supermarkets had to pack the food up in a special way to give it to the charities, it would increase their costs. As a result, supermarkets would probably raise their prices, so it would be more expensive for the rest of us to do our shopping.

(D) _____ Although I think that the French made this law for good reasons, in my view, it would be better to allow supermarkets to decide for themselves what to do with their unsold food.

1 Read the essay and match paragraphs A–D with topic sentences 1–5. There is one extra topic sentence.

  1   On the one hand, this may seem like a good idea. _____

  2   Supermarkets often throw away large amounts of food waste. _____

  3   To sum up, I do not believe that all countries should do the same as France. _____

  4   Supermarkets are businesses, and they cannot afford to give people free food. _____

  5   On the other hand, is it right for the government to interfere in business in this way? _____

2 Which of these arguments does the writer use?

  1 For
    a We should help people who are hungry.
    b It is better to give unsold food to people who can use it.
    c It is a waste of money to throw away good food.
    d Businesses should do something to help poor people.
    e Food waste is bad for the environment.

  2 Against
    a Giving food to charities requires extra work for supermarkets and may increase prices.
    b Supermarkets should use better systems to reduce food waste.
    c We should give poor people the food they need – not just the food nobody else wants.
    d This system would encourage people not to work.
    e Supermarkets should be free to do what they like with the food that belongs to them.

3 Complete these topic sentences for the essay with ideas from exercise 2 or your own ideas.

  1 The main advantage of _____.

  2 However, one disadvantage _____.

  3 On the one hand, _____.

  4 On the other hand, _____.

  5 To sum up, _____.

4 Rewrite the final three paragraphs of the essay above and reach a different conclusion.

  • Use at least one new argument for and one new argument against.
  • Start each paragraph with a topic sentence and a linking phrase.
  • Remember to use formal language.

WRITING: Writing a review

ACTIVITY VACATION IN FRANCE

I went on this vacation with a group of friends. According to the website, it was going to be the adventure of a lifetime in one of the most gorgeous parts of France, surrounded by fantastic mountain scenery. In fact, in the end, it wasn't really an adventure vacation at all.

On Day One, we were supposed to go white water rafting in a huge canyon. Sadly, because of a storm the night before, the water was too dangerous, and we ended up going for a short walk, instead. On Day Three, the plan was to go skiing on a nearby glacier, where there's snow all year round. However, our driver clearly didn't know the way, and it took us so long to get there that we only had an hour for skiing by the time we finally reached the glacier.

This vacation should have been perfect for a group of young people like us, but, actually, it was a big disappointment. I wouldn't recommend it to anyone.

HIKING IN NEPAL

My brother and I went hiking in Nepal in the summer. It was something I had always wanted to do. Obviously, I had expected it to be tough, but I don't think I realized just how exhausted I would be at the end of each day! However, I improved quickly, and by Day Four, I was feeling in much better shape and was really enjoying the experience. By the end of the vacation, I didn't want to stop walking!

The vacation brochure had warned us that the food wouldn't be of restaurant quality because everything had to be carried. Surprisingly, it was actually pretty good. We were always hungry from walking, and the meals were both tasty and large!

This vacation is perfect for anyone looking for a real adventure. But I would recommend getting in better shape than I was before you go, and it wouldn't be suitable for anyone with health problems.

1 Read the two reviews and match 1–6 with what the reviewers say (a–j).

1 expectations of the vacation in France   ____ ____
2 expectations of the vacation in Nepal   ____ ____
3 what the vacation in France was really like ____ ____
4 what the vacation in Nepal was really like ____ ____
5 who would enjoy the vacation in France ____
6 who would enjoy the vacation in Nepal ____

a very adventurous
b no one
c problems with the activities
d physically hard
e rather boring
f extremely tiring
g good food
h people that are in good shape and healthy
i simple food
j beautiful scenery

2 Complete the sentences with your own ideas for vacation reviews.

1 Our plane was delayed, and we didn't land until after midnight. Luckily, _____.
2 We had expected to have a view of the beach. Unfortunately, _____.
3 I thought a vacation in Japan would be extremely expensive. Surprisingly, _____.
4 The hotel room was cold and dirty. Obviously, _____.
5 We weren't able to visit the rainforest because of the hurricane. Hopefully, _____.
6 The website showed pictures of happy families playing in the sun. Sadly, _____.
7 It wouldn't have been safe to go into the jungle alone. Clearly, _____.

3 Write a review of a visit to somewhere with beautiful or interesting scenery.

Before you start, write down ideas for things you will say were good or bad. Remember to include the following:

• what your expectations were before you went
• what it was really like
• who would or wouldn't enjoy the experience
• at least two adverbs of attitude (unfortunately, hopefully, etc.)

58 St Aldates
Oxford
OX1 1ST
United Kingdom

ISBN: 978-84-668-2648-8
© Richmond / Santillana Global S.L. 2017

Publishing Director: Deborah Tricker
Publisher: Simone Foster
Media Publisher: Sue Ashcroft
Workbook Publisher: Luke Baxter
Content Developer: Stephanie Bremner
Editors: Peter Anderson, Debra Emmett, Helen Ward, Tom Hadland, Eleanor Clements, Ruth Cox, Fiona Hunt, Kate Mellersh, Fiona Hunt, Helen Wendholt
Americanization: Deborah Goldblatt
Proofreaders: Bruce Wade, Tas Cooper, Shannon Neill
Design Manager: Lorna Heaslip
Cover Design: This Ain't Rock'n'Roll, London
Design & Layout: Lorna Heaslip, Oliver Hutton, ColArt Design
Photo Researcher: Magdalena Mayo
Learning Curve video: Mannic Media
Audio Production: Eastern Sky Studios
App Development: The Distance

We would also like to thank the following people for their valuable contribution to writing and developing the material:
Alastair Lane, Bob McLarty, Brigit Viney, Pamela Vittorio (Video Script Writer), Belen Fernandez (App Project Manager), Eleanor Clements (App Content Creator)

We would like to thank all those who have given their kind permission to reproduce material for this book:

Illustration:
Simon Clare; Dermot Flynn c/o Dutch Uncle; Guillaume Gennet c/o Lemonade; John Goodwin; The Boy FitzHammond c/o NB Illustration; Douglas Strachan at Strachangray Creative

Photos:
J. Jaime; S. Enríquez; 123RF; ALAMY/WENN Ltd., PhotoAlto sas, AF archive, HO Images, Chronicle, BSIP SA, B Christopher, Lev Dolgachov, Morey Milbradt, Richard Levine, Kevin Su, Rob Watkins, epa european pressphoto agency b.v., cineclassico, Aflo Co. Ltd., Mark Eden, Photo Japan, REUTERS, Mark phillips, Peterforsberg, Jorge Peréz, ilpo musto, Design Pics Inc, ZUMA Press, Inc., Glasshouse Images, MBI, TGSPHOTO, CoverSpot Photography, Entertainment Pictures, Allstar Picture Library, Tewin Kijthamrongworakul, Tribune Content Agency LLC, Pictorial Press Ltd, Caryn Becker; BBC; BNPS (BOURNEMOUTH NEWS & PICTURE SERVICE)

Rachel Adams, Steve Way; GETTY IMAGES SALES SPAIN/ Photodisc/Thinkstock, Photos.com Plus, Thinkstock; GTRESONLINE; I. PREYSLER; ISTOCKPHOTO/Getty Images Sales Spain; JOHN FOXX IMAGES; REX SHUTTERSTOCK/ FOX/Genre Movies, Page Images, Sipa Press, Silverhub, Galvan/AP, Ray Tang; SHUTTERSTOCK/Rex; SHUTTERSTOCK NETHERLANDS,B.V.; SOUTHWEST NEWS; wikipedia/ Ed g2s; Michael Parsons; Pedroromero2; Neil Douglas; Rockford Register Star and rrstar.com; COAST Collective Architecture Studio; Amos Magliocco/Eric Nguyen; courtsey of Vic Armstrong; Carroll County Sheriff; Project Monsoon, School of the Art Institute of Chicago; SERIDEC PHOTOIMAGENES CD; ARCHIVO SANTILLANA; GETTY IMAGES SALES SPAIN/ Westend61; ISTOCKPHOTO; Prats i Camps; ALAMY/Photo 12, Sylvie Bouchard, Dinendra Haria, Peter Wheeler, age fotostock, travelstock44, Dave Stevenson, Moviestore collection Ltd, Jim West, Mikael Damkier,Nathaniel Noir, PURPLE MARBLES, Matthew Chattle, jaileybug,ONOKY - Photononstop, Newscast Online Limited, PJF Military Collection, Kerry Dunstone, FORGET Patrick/SAGAPHOTO.COM, Chuck Pefley; GETTY IMAGES SALES SPAIN/Thinkstock; ISTOCKPHOTO/Getty Images Sales Spain; ARCHIVO SANTILLANA

Cover Photo: iStockphoto/Getty Images Sales Spain

Texts:
p.48 Adapted from 'Fabrice Muamba: how I went from professional footballer to journalist' by Hannah Friend, Guardian Professional, 11 June 2014. Copyright Guardian News & Media Ltd 2016.

p.16 Adapted from 'Meet Steve Way - England's unlikeliest athlete for the Commonwealth Games' by Sean Ingle, theguardian.com, 31 May 2014. Copyright Guardian News & Media Ltd 2016.

We would like to thank the following reviewers for their valuable feedback which has made Personal Best possible. We extend our thanks to the many teachers and students not mentioned here.
Brad Bawtinheimer, Manuel Hidalgo, Paulo Dantas, Diana Bermúdez, Laura Gutiérrez, Hardy Griffin, Angi Conti, Christopher Morabito, Hande Kokce, Jorge Lobato, Leonardo Mercato, Mercilinda Ortiz, Wendy López

Printed in Brazil by Forma Certa Gráfica Digital
Lote: 800.418